THE WOMB
OF SPACE

Contributions in Afro-American and African Studies
Series Advisers: John W. Blassingame and Henry Louis Gates, Jr.

The Afro-Yankees: Providence's Black Community in the Antebellum Era
Robert J. Cottrol

A Case of Black and White: Northern Volunteers and the Southern Freedom Summers, 1964-1965
Mary Aickin Rothschild

Gatekeepers of Black Culture: Black-Owned Book Publishing in the United States, 1817-1981
Donald Franklin Joyce

The Craft of an Absolute Winner: Characterization and Narratology in the Novels of Machado de Assis
Maria Luisa Nunes

Black Marriage and Family Therapy
Edited by Constance E. Obudho

THE WOMB OF SPACE

The Cross-Cultural Imagination

WILSON HARRIS

CONTRIBUTIONS IN AFRO-AMERICAN AND
AFRICAN STUDIES, NUMBER 73

GP

GREENWOOD PRESS
WESTPORT, CONNECTICUT • LONDON, ENGLAND

Library of Congress Cataloging in Publication Data

Harris, Wilson.
    The womb of space.

    (Contributions in Afro-American and African studies,
ISSN 0069-9624 ; no. 73)
    Bibliography: p.
    Includes index.

    1. Literature, Modern—20th century—History and
criticism. 2. Caribbean Area. I. Title. II. Series.
PN771.H23 1983   809'.04   83-1639
ISBN 0-313-23774-3 (lib. bdg.)

Library of Congress Catalog Card Number: 83-1639
ISBN: 0-313-23774-3
ISSN: 0069-9624

First published in 1983

Greenwood Press
A division of Congressional Information Service, Inc.
88 Post Road West
Westport, Connecticut 06881

Printed in the United States of America

10 9 8 7 6 5 4 3 2 1

FOR MARGARET,

JOSEPH AND JOHANNA JONES

and

(in memory of)

CHARLES T. DAVIS

Contents

Series Foreword

The paucity of creative and scholarly works available for library and classroom use remains a crucial barrier to the adequate study of African and Afro-American arts and letters. Despite a flood of hastily conceived and rashly executed monograph and bibliographical series that ostensibly meant to address this quandry, students, scholars, and librarians agree that African and Afro-American materials continue to be either inadequate as research tools or, more often, simply unavailable.

Despite the intention of well-meaning publishers and eager Afro-Americanists, the 1880 lament of the black critic, Richard T. Greener, retains its poignancy as an account of knowledge of black arts and letters: "It would be interesting, were it not painful, to observe how little even educated Americans, judging from articles in current literature, know of the capacity, disposition, achievements, services, or sacrifices of the Negro in general and the Negro-American in particular." The American academy has only a limited notion of the manner in which black writers and scholars have structured their responses to the complex fate of institutionalized racial and economic discrimination. Nor does the academy have a sufficient idea of the peculiar manner in which black texts respond to considerations raised in other related texts—the responses themselves constituting an aspect of intellectual history. What's more, no publishing venture has systematically addressed this problem by commissioning major Africanists and Afro-Americanists to prepare sophisticated studies on the vast and challenging subject of the black arts and letters.

To sharpen the definition of African and Afro-American Studies and to present a more coherent view of the continuum of black thought and action, a new departure is necessary. This series is designed to fill this need. Often inter-disciplinary and cross-cultural, it seeks to address not only the complexities of the cultural and aesthetic confrontation of black cultures with non-black ones, but also the nature and function of African and Afro-American arts and letters themselves.

* * *

Wilson Harris is one of the most prolific novelists writing in any language. Harris has published at least fourteen novels, two collections of short stories, two books of poems, and two books of critical essays, in addition to this collection. Even more so than most creative writers, Harris is concerned to theorize about the nature and function of art generally, and about the nature and function of black art more especially. Above all else, Wilson Harris is concerned with the relation between the artist and his or her sense of a community, or communities. He frequently depicts this concern in his novels in the figure of a surveyor, Harris's favorite character. But Harris's sense of language in the novel, and of the novel's central element, the event, is profoundly—indeed, densely—metaphorical. Myth and metaphor determine Harris's lexicon and his mode of representation in the novel. Perhaps not surprisingly, Harris's criticism reflects this affinity with myth.

Perhaps because of the political uses to which black literature traditionally has been put, the dominant mode of fictional representation is "realism," or its aesthetic extreme, "naturalism." In this sort of fiction, we presuppose a more or less *direct* relation between "the real world" and the fictional "world" of the text; indeed, some writers and critics argue that the function of all committed art is to mirror, in a text, the social or political, or economic relationships that obtain in society, in a hypothetical one-to-one relationship. This sort of writing is often called "social realism."

Wilson Harris is not a social realist writer. He is, rather, a writer whose primary concern would seem to be with the "reality" of *language* itself, rather than with reflecting *directly* material or political relationships. No critic puts this better than does C.L.R. James, whose essay, "Wilson Harris and the Existentialist Doctrine," is a reading of two of Harris's novels (*Palace of the Peacock* and *The Secret Ladder*) within the philosophical tradition best exemplified by Jaspers, Heidegger, and the Jean-Paul Sartre of *Being and Nothingness*.

James argues that Heidegger's definition of *dasein*, of "being there," is at the center of Harris's creative project. As James puts it, "the *dasein*, the 'being there,' is an uncovering of the truth of Being that exists. Not beings but Being itself." But "being" and "existence" are remarkably distinct states; the movement between them is Harris's great topos, his undergirding, repeated theme—a theme represented by, in, and through language-use. As James continues:

mountains are, horses are, books are, but only man *exists* and the source of man's existence is not only the *dasein*. The means he uses to find what he is finding out, to live an authentic existence, is language, and I have seen that nowhere stated as sharply as Harris states it.

It is this particular concern with language that most distinguishes Harris's creative and critical enterprise; to allow James to conclude: "Language. Language is not a tool; politics is a tool, painting is a tool, scientific procedures are tools of mankind, but language is not. In Heidegger's [and Harris's] view man lives a human life because of language. Without that he would . . . not be a human being. . . ." Harris, in other words, represents his characters' movement from the "inauthentic" to the "authentic" existence as a process of *language-use*. In this sense, Harris is not only a thoroughly "modern" writer; he is "post-modern." As he puts the matter in "Spirit of the Fall,"

Clouds experience youth and age when they glance so quickly across the earth, and fall to the deep world around in tiny raindrops and mist. Skies clear and vision finds the torrent sparkling in the sun.

The splendors, limits, and ironies of *consciousness* are Wilson Harris's great concerns.

Concern with the representation of consciousness is most certainly in evidence in Harris's literary criticism of the sort collected in this book. Throughout these essays—meditations, really, upon the critical and the creative *process* themselves— Harris is concerned to show the fundamental unity of the human community, both by underscoring repeated patterns of symbol-making or "figuration" in the world's cultures and art and by revealing the movement from unawareness to consciousness as depicted in the mythic symbol. By discussing texts from the American, Latin American, and European literary traditions, Harris analyzes that quality which "mythical" novels share in common. This book will be especially useful for students and scholars of comparative literature and especially black literature. It is also an indispensable guide to Harris's understanding of his own novels and their import and testifies to Wilson Harris's consciousness of the essence and purpose of great art.

John W. Blassingame
Henry Louis Gates, Jr.

Acknowledgments

The opportunity to undertake research for this book I owe mainly to the John Simon Guggenheim Memorial Foundation which awarded me a Fellowship for the year 1972-73.

I am also grateful to the University of Texas at Austin; Yale University; the University of Aarhus, Denmark; the University of East Anglia; Newcastle University, Australia; and the University of Mysore, India, where I spent guest lectureships and fellowships over the past eight years and spoke on some of the themes presented in this study. I benefited from the response of members of faculty and students, and also was glad for the opportunity to experience some of the physical and social landscapes that engage the imagination of writers whose novels and poems appear in this cross-cultural exploration.

Introduction

I shall attempt, in this exploration, to bring into play certain disregarded yet exciting pathways into the reality of traditions that bear upon cross-cultural capacities for genuine change in communities beset by complex dangers and whose antecedents are diverse.

Science fiction makes no bones about the status of writers such as Jules Verne and H. G. Wells whose space fantasies are now technologically respectable. Aldous Huxley's *Brave New World* is already with us in blue-prints for genetic engineering. George Orwell's *1984* exists apparently not only in the files of Big Brother but in telephone taps and other ghostly signals.

There is a tendency to glorify such writers as prophets but what is at stake is grounded less in prophecy, I would suggest, and more significantly in the trickster natures of freedom and fate, the comedy of freedom masking itself in claustrophobic ritual or vehicle. Despite the strength of nihilism in the West and in the so-called Third World, it is arguable that society is approaching in uncertain degree a horizon of sensibility upon which a capacity exists to begin to transform claustrophobic ritual by cross-cultural imaginations that bear upon the future through mutations of the monolithic character of conquistadorial legacies of civilisation, and that one is not wholly circumscribed by 'genetic robot' or Orwellian nemesis.

The true character of cosmic freedom is obscure, yet that

obscurity or darkness may bring to imaginative fiction and poetry a luminous paradox, depth and tone, within the frailty of the human person in the backcloth—yet live tapestry—of the universe that is appearing to the mind of science, a universe of black holes, of neutrinos, of nameless entities named 'quarks' by Joycean scientists; a frailty that can be exploited mercilessly, yet is so elusive in essence it resists conscription, it matches itself by subtle fissures of illumination within the prisonhouse of existence.

The subtlety of such illumination inevitably reaches forward and backward into the distance of time, into futurity as dimension— complex dimension that seems objective yet confesses to anthropomorphic elements in creature and creator, in every fable of evolution or non-evolution within the biases of particular generations.

The subtlety of such illumination is woven into the living imagination to make an intuitive leap and to come abreast, as in a dream, of the secrets of potentiality. Those secrets do suggest immaterial and untamable foundations to the cosmos or to a universe composed of fabrics of mobility akin to thought (if I may paraphrase the metaphysics of a great astronomer) but more immediately and tragically they conspire with the popular addiction to material dread and exploitation of species and resources, and to brute fantasy.

This addiction is not surprising. Our grasp of time tends— everyone knows—to incorporate tragic proportions or determined futures and to overlook unspectacular resources of futurity and imagination that may alter perception *through* and away from fixed habit, greed and monoliths of terror.

Perhaps somewhere along the line of life in creation's hand that shaped Adam out of fabulous mud, life 'prophesied' its coming in hieroglyphic atmospheres, metaphoric vehicles and sculptures drawn upon sky and earth into a museum of gods, until vehicle or constellation became an obsession in the wake or arousal of the human imagination, and the nail of space invited a further hammer to equate walled circumstance with the mysterious genesis of life itself pitted against the greatest odds and adverse environments.

In our late twentieth-century age, grappling with fuel crises and the stubborn motor car as with ritual property of all kinds, one may with hindsight glimmeringly perceive that vehicles of genesis, that human cultures tend to symbolise into absolute structuralism, may possess ironic textures to mirror apparently non-existent life in subordination to ruling unconsciousness across aeons of matter and space that are the geologic equivalent to blind cultural habit by which we are governed.

And, as a consequence, a tendency exists to turn away from original creation or unspectacular genesis in-or-through stubborn pages of fate and to invest in a fortress book armed against menaces to survival; in becoming glimmeringly aware of this predilection-in-range-and-depth (matched by intuitive fissures of illumination and subtle transformations of bias) we may look afresh with somewhat shattered yet curiously liberated eyes at the living museum of creation, the repetitive logic that sustains our grimmest expectations or fears of unfreedom.

Imaginative sensibility is uniquely equipped by forces of dream and paradox to mirror the inimitable activity of subordinated psyche; inimitable in that no art of total capture or subordination of originality within formula exists despite appearances. Thus the unity or density of original expression, in a work of profound imagination, is paradox; it is both a cloak for, and a dialogue with, eclipses of live 'otherness' that seek to break through in a new light and tone expressive of layers of reality. Sometimes this combination and breakthrough—in Edgar Allan Poe's *Arthur Gordon Pym* for example—is schizophrenic or the source of abortive mutiny (as if driven by a subversive myth of self—a dangerous sub-text of the imagination) within an over-text of ego-historical command the writer reveres and obeys.

Our exploration starts with a series of reflections on William Faulkner's *Intruder in the Dust*. This will help, I think, to make clear at the outset some of the tormenting issues, yet exciting possibilities, in a perception of cross-cultural capacity. It is unlikely, as we shall see, that Faulkner was aware how strangely his imagination had been pulled in this novel into coincidence with black theatre of psyche, the *expédition* or *l'envoi morts* that Alfred Métraux defines.[1]

Let me dwell a little on the phenomenon of otherness that moves in the novel yet remains curiously beyond Faulkner's vision, so to speak. Had he seen it—had the life of heterogeneity, in unconscious or intuitive dialogue with his creativity, come home to him—he would have been driven, I think, to revise the one-sided moral conclusions built into the closing premises of the novel.

What perhaps I should say now is that the phenomenon of otherness borders on the validity of mental images as distinct from intellectual conclusions; I am reminded of Alastair Hannay's argument in which he demonstrates how valid mental images are and how misleading is the ground Ryle, Shorter, Sartre and other philosophers have adopted. Hannay says, "Disentangling the conclusion from its premises . . . gives phenomena a chance to breathe more freely and speak for themselves."[2] The remark could well apply to the concluding sermon of fortress homogeneity in *Intruder in the Dust* that extinguishes intuitive dialogue between dominant 'one' and largely invisible 'other', despite earlier phenomena in the novel that had begun to illumine a cross-cultural medium within a deeper and stranger unity of sensibility *through* and beyond polarised structures.

It is necessary to make clear within the fabric of imaginative exploration we shall pursue that homogeneity is a biological hypothesis that relates all mankind to a basic or primordial ancestor, but as a cultural model, exercised by a ruling ethnic group, it tends to become an organ of conquest and division because of *imposed* unity that actually subsists on the suppression of others.

The paradox of cultural heterogeneity, or cross-cultural capacity, lies in the evolutionary thrust it restores to orders of the imagination, the ceaseless dialogue it inserts between hardened conventions and eclipsed or half-eclipsed otherness, within an intuitive self that moves endlessly into flexible patterns, arcs or bridges of community.

I return to Alfred Métraux and the coincidence that resides in the corpse of Vinson Gowrie and Haitian *expédition*. For that hidden *rapport* between Faulkner's intuitive imagination and Lucas Beauchamp's anonymous black kith and kin in the Caribbean gives an original twist to the drama of psychical awakening from nightmare programme of the past in the future, the ceaseless nightmare of history.

Métraux writes, "The most fearful practice in the black arts—the one which the ordinary people are always talking about, is the sending of the dead [*l'envoi morts* or *expédition*]. Whoever has become the prey of one or more dead people sent against him begins to grow thin, spit blood and is soon dead. The laying on of this spell is always attended by fatal results unless it is diagnosed in time and a capable *hungan* succeeds in making the dead let go."

That the corpse of Vinson Gowrie may be interpreted as ceaseless nightmare of history or institutionalized spectre of prejudice "sent against" Lucas Beauchamp enriches the depth-potential of *Intruder in the Dust* and suggests an activity of image beyond given verbal convention into non-verbal arts of the imagination in the womb of cultural space as though an *unstructured force* arbitrates or mediates between articulate or verbal signs and silent or eclipsed voices of nemesis in folk religions whose masks or sculptures subsist upon implicit metaphors of death-in-life, life-in-death. We shall explore these provocative considerations through the body of selected fictions and poems in this study.

Our exploration acquires backward sweep in moving us from the twentieth century into Edgar Allan Poe's nineteenth-century *Arthur Gordon Pym* in which lies submerged a dialogue with pre-Columbian myth and its bearing on 'magical corpse' investitures. We shall return to the twentieth century with a heightened awareness of the carnival elements evoked in Ralph Ellison's *Invisible Man*, Jean Toomer's *Cane*, Juan Rulfo's Mexican *Pedro Páramo*, Jay Wright's *Double Invention of Komo* and Jean Rhys's Anglo-Caribbean *Wide Sargasso Sea*. These fictions and poems in turn are the threshold into a body of contrasting works by writers such as Paule Marshall, Aimé Césaire, Derek Walcott, Edward Brathwaite (from the Americas), Mervyn Peake, Emma Tennant, Claude Simon, Raja Rao and Zulfikar Ghose (from Europe and Asia).

A word about the selection of novels and poems in this study. Selection is necessarily restricted and, in some instances, the comment on novels or poems under reflection is brief, but my prime responsibility lay with the elaboration of gateways into the largely submerged territory of the imagination. Other fictions may well have been chosen, and the intention indeed is to imply that the ground of active reflection over which we move is a ceaseless, strangely objective threshold into apparently incompatible arts of existence around the globe. In this particular study, and within the stresses of a cross-cultural exploration rarely undertaken by readers or critics, I had no al-

ternative but to limit my selection in order to highlight variables
of dialogue that tend to be suppressed in so-called normal clas-
sifications of fiction and poetry within regional scholarship.

In addition to the stresses on variables of dialogue I was af-
fected by a quest for works of the imagination that border on
alchemies of image and word. That borderline gives us scope,
I am sure, to conceive of criteria that are neither monolithic
nor nihilist, but—I must confess—the growth of nihilism and
totalitarianism in the twentieth century world makes such a
hopeful view or vision of impartial criteria a complex one. I
have in no way sought to bypass the difficulties in specific works
that do not lend themselves immediately to such criteria or interpretation, though they may still assist us in extreme perspective with other imaginations.

Perhaps the major obstacle we shall encounter is the ambiguity
of the muses in a world of debased psyche. It is, I think, of great
interest to perceive not only 'blocked muses' (as I have called them)
but states of 'psychical marriage' between unconscious bridegroom
and apparently doomed bride, 'psychical widowhood' as well
(when one party 'lives' like an ornament of historical relationship
yet 'dies' to the other's essential being) in characterisations created
by writers as diverse in temperament and art as Jean Rhys, Paule
Marshall, Raja Rao, Patrick White and Djuna Barnes.

Exile is the ground of live fossil and sensuous memory within
uncertain roots that are threaded into legacies of transplantation in
Caribbean poetry, correspondences with certain African and
European poets. We reflect on the addiction to protest realism,
complex philistinism and the allurements of self-pity that fascinate
the Caribbean mind even as we begin all over again the pursuit of
enduring cross-cultural spirit in arts of dialogue with unsuspected
and supportive myth.

THE WOMB
OF SPACE

ONE

Reflections on *Intruder in the Dust* in a Cross-cultural Complex

The Fall

Intruder in the Dust is a comedy of psyche and the implications that reside in such a theme (or combination of themes) tend to be overlooked by critics who indict the novel for its "provincialism" or "rhetoric."

It is true that a case can be made against the novel for hardened convention that is akin to provincial stasis, but once we begin to see the action of dark comedy within the narrative, a strange light, I find, arises through which "provincialism" relinquishes its powers and a body of harlequin features—rooted in many cultures—comes into play and points to a universe of unsuspected diversity, correspondence and potential.

Likewise what seems unnatural rhetoric at first sight in the narrative acquires a capacity to illuminate patterns of claustrophobia which reveal themselves first as buried premises, then almost simultaneously as heightened premises that are reluctant to come forward or upward as if they resist the excavation of imagination that acts upon them in the soil of place, as if they are conscious of being unreal in being raised from a state of long eclipse into the bewildering lights and pressures of consciousness.

It is necessaary to note the curious anthropomorphism at work in the novel. The writer appears to create the premises he depicts but is also created, so to speak, by them. His premises are *alive*, they are reluctant to be raised to consciousness. This comedy of thrust and counter-thrust between the writer who makes a world of peculiar sensations and is also *made*, in some degree, by the world he makes (as if the world he makes is truly alive in its own right) is the substance of rhetoric Faulkner employs. This thrust—and intuitive return thrust—with its wealth of perspective, tends to be blocked and flattened, in some parts of the novel and as the novel draws to a close, by a prickly regionalism or fortress homogeneity, exercised by Faulkner's hierarchy of intentions. This imposes a barren philosophical climax that gives some weight to the charges that have been levelled against the work.

It is only proper and fair to summarise those charges by quoting an actual passage, representative of adverse critical opinion, from Edmond L. Volpe's study of William Faulkner.

[This] is his most provincial novel. His analysis of the Southern consciousness illuminates the complex psychological and social forces that make the intelligent white Southerner a unique phenomenon of the twentieth century. But because Faulkner treats his subject as a special problem—everyone not born a white Southerner is an Outlander—the significance and value of his book as art is minimal. Of even more importance, perhaps, in accounting for the failure of the novel as a work of art is Faulkner's assumption of the role of spokesman for the South. He sacrifices his art to social analysis and preaching. The result is a propaganda novel. The melodramatic plot in which two boys—a Negro and a white—and an old woman open a grave to prove that the Negro, Lucas Beauchamp, about to be lynched for the murder of a white man, is innocent, is too slight a story to maintain the weight of rhetoric Faulkner heaps upon it.[1]

The tasks of a critic are manifold and difficult, especially when it becomes necessary to descend with the creative imagination into half-excavated, half-reluctant, living strata of place that lie under reinforcements of habit or convention or fortress institution that may parade itself as moral imperative. But it is clear that Volpe makes no effort to grasp the irrational coherence—the capacity for fictions within fictions, truths within truths all 'writing' each other in being 'written' by each other, that breaches conventional logic and gives the novel its complicated power and focus. Thus, in my judgement, he is drawn into an astonishing under-estimation of a complex and demanding art in which the emphasis shifts from ruling ego to intuitive layers of self or selves, and a transformed mosaic of community comes into play. That transformation lapses into misgiving, retreat, hollow moralising and hollow spokesmanship for the South at stages of Faulkner's narrative, but its significance is nevertheless profound and far-reaching.

When I say 'intuitive' layers of self, in contradistinction to 'ruling' ego, I mean a darkened psychic concentration that so pools itself it becomes an interior mirror reflecting outer activity. It loses the biased rituals of material property in favor of kinship with images that cease to be passive or submerged; instead each image is an apparent catalyst of discovery, it acts upon the falling or ascending weight of a subtle imagination immersed in what it appears to describe.

Each image, therefore, confesses to textures which make paradoxically real a universe ceaselessly subject to qualities of alteration within creator and created, a universe that can never be taken for granted as dead matter; objective status is eternally flawed, eternally aware of breached limits, eternally susceptible therefore to an organ of wholeness that is never achieved (or identified permanently in nature or in psyche) but is paradoxically there nevertheless at the heart of a creation in which pressures of dialogue, spheres of duality, exist between creator and created. Both are, in a context of human frailty and imagination, partial conceptions within a riddle of unfathomable being or timeless moment.

This issue will emerge in a variety of ways within the womb of space and labyrinth we pursue. Its occurrence in *Intruder in the Dust* thrusts the reader, at times without warning as if to invite a 'lived' and 'living' experience of suppressed, still momentous, dialogue, into the peculiar *breathlessness, immobilisation* and *suffocation* that accompany claustrophobia—a claustrophobia that looms early in the novel, and secretes a precipice of emotion down which young Charles Mallison falls, to play a crucial, nervous role in coming abreast of the rising premises of otherness within an excavation of psyche and place.

The psychical consequences of that fall are threaded into himself, into his companion Aleck Sander and indeed into the entire cast of the novel, by degrees of implication and casualty woven into the texture of the narrative. In the first place, the formidable narcissistic core of the society Faulkner immerses us in seems phenomenally bruised in young Mallison's fall. This multiple bruise—inner and outer—that unites him to others is a tribute to his youth, his capacity for fantasy, and to the irrational and intensely human awareness built into the crevices of childhood, of layers of imagination he shares with the entire community, however hidden such layers are by the carapace of institution or complacent habit.

The shock inflicted on complacent institution by the consequences of the fall is, in substantial part, a clue to Faulkner's irony (unconscious irony, I would think) in wedding falling/rising place to the riddle of consciousness. The precipitous fall is an uplift in terrain, an uplift of figures who loom into him with such astonishing exaggeration of contour and paradoxical exactitude that he can no longer remain blind to them as in the past. One exaggerated contour is as much part of the illusion and blow of exactitude within the opening eye; descent defines ascent of new birth, new awareness, and vice versa. Both are native extremes to each other, unconsciousness to the precarious and stretched limits of consciousness. And therein lies the spirit of the paradoxical museum of the world embodied in stasis that becomes unpredictably active; the fossil of age begins to live in persons who seem to wear their very skins like close-fitting yet interchangeable costumes of vertical destiny and abrupt sensation, mirrored features, one in the other, black in white.

The abruptness with which they slide into and out of unconscious habit is a revelation of the vertigo of exactitude, illusory exactitude, humour of exactitude, and this undermining of stasis—a stasis which parades as the exact truth of tradition—leads to built-in evolutions, long eclipsed or forgotten, that exist within the most hardened property or consensus of fate.

In that disclosure of eclipsed evolutions lies the dawn, the thread of dawn, woven into potential heterogeneity, and arching through European, African and pre-Columbian hidden antecedents to which Faulkner refers—"the whole sum of their ancestral horror and scorn and fear of Indian and Chinese and Mexican and Carib and Jew . . ." in the psyche of place.[2] It is a darkened illumination or obscure light, as much a source of dread as of hope, and this fittingly becomes a symbol in itself of overshadowed or diminished poetry that lurks in the novel, and gives to the prose an awkwardness at times, an awkward and pregnant illumination of consciousness that seems oddly right in drawing one into the consequences of Charles Mallison's fall and its extensions into the entire community, the living and the dead.

It was cold that morning . . . and the standing water . . . was skimmed with ice . . . scintillant like fairy glass and from the first farmyard they passed . . . came the windless tang of woodsmoke and they could see the black iron pots already steaming while women in the sun-bonnets still of summer or men's old felt hats and long men's overcoats stoked wood under them and the men with crokersack aprons tied with wire over their over-alls whetted knives . . . by nightfall the whole land would be hung with their *spectral intact tallow coloured empty carcasses immobilised by the heels in frantic running full tilt at the centre of the earth.*

. . . Aleck Sander and Edmonds' boy with tapsticks and he with the gun . . . went down through the park to the creek where Edmonds' boy knew the footlog was and he didn't know how it happened, something a girl might have been . . . excused for doing but nobody else, half-way over the footlog . . . when *all of a sudden the known familiar sunny winter earth was upside down and flat on his face and still holding the gun he was rushing not away from the earth but away from the bright sky* [italics mine].[3]

Mallison falls into the creek. A sense of bulk and protuberance, the trade of slaughterhouse in farmyard and factory he has passed on his way to the creek, casts its shadow over him like a pregnant design, an exaggerated contour, illusory exactitude, yet his reflection on "a girl [who] might have been excused" sustains something of the smothered graces of the half-drowned, shot rabbit he has himself become. They were on their way to hunt and kill rabbits but young Mallison himself falls into the 'grave of the creek.'

Aleck Sander thrusts a pole into the creek but it is the iron-faced black commanding Lucas Beauchamp—proud and pitiless as the white farmers on the land—who looms out of nowhere, it seems, and takes charge of the operation: "and he could remember still, the breaking ice . . . *his clothes like soft cold lead which he didn't move in* . . . he saw two feet in gum boots . . . the legs; the over-alls . . . *a Negro man with an axe on his shoulder* . . . Lucas

Beauchamp . . . watching him without pity [or] commiseration
. . . not even surprise: just watching him [italics mine]."[4]

In that passage, as in the previous quotation, the sense of
exaggerated contour and paradoxical exactitude addresses us, but
above all one begins to perceive, I would suggest, an intuitive
threshold into *expédition* or *l'envoi morts* within broad daylight
theatrical narrative.

The force of that intuitive threshold cannot be but marked and
peculiar—in its hidden seismic pressure—on the prose style of
Intruder in the Dust. It is bright yet dark upheaval, day yet night.
The precipice of emotion down which Charles falls is in the nature
of a dream or a suspended contour of night in broad daylight,
"soft cold lead [in] which he didn't move" yet "carcasses immobilized
. . . full tilt at the centre of the earth."

That contour of dream triggers both human rabbit and pregnant
execution within the womb of space. The trigger lodges itself in the
looming presence of Lucas Beauchamp standing above the 'grave
of the creek" with an axe on his shoulder. The pitiless gaze he di-
rects upon hapless rabbit or victim of the hunt in metaphoric
senses differs little from the severe detachment he is to evince not
long afterwards in the novel, when he stands not with an axe
but with a gun in his hand over the dead body of Vinson Gowrie,
and finds himself as a consequence not only accused of murder but
threatened by an outraged community, outraged convention, for
his insolence to and disregard of enshrined patterns of behaviour.

He has aroused the fire of institutional bias, the sorcery of hate
enshrined in institutional 'corpse', sacred vengeance or "sent dead"
in Voodoo vocabulary. The two scenes are linked together, the
scene at the creek and the scene over the sacred body of a dead
Gowrie from Beat Four where the Gowrie clan rules, to symbolise
territorial imperative or regime.

Young Mallison's fall in broad daylight winter morning theatre
possesses another hidden underside or premise that comes to light
in the nightsky, so to speak, of a culture, in constellations hidden
by the deed of the sun. That thread embodies the mantle of the
hungan that is to fall upon young Charles Mallison, Aleck Sander
and elderly Miss Habersham (whose relationship to Lucas's family
we shall discuss later).

Charles knew, when Beauchamp was accused of shooting Vinson

Gowrie in cold blood, that he too would have subscribed to that view which rested on daylight appearance—on the gun in Lucas's hand as he stood over the body of the murdered man, as he had stood before with an axe on his shoulder over a mesmerised creature in a creek—but Charles had been changed by his fall into the theatre of a grave like one masked, as in a dream, by his own slain pride, slain habit. He had felt himself bound to Lucas then by resentment and awe as he emerged from the creek. He had been confused by the other's pitiless gaze, by the uncompromising spirit in which he had been shepherded into Lucas's house, tended and fed there.

Who was black Lucas, he had wondered in confusion, to behave as if he were white, pitiless and proud? We shall return to the ground of Lucas's hospitality later; I mention it now to endorse young Mallison's double sensation of receiving a blow, woven into his fall, that dismantled Southern racial protocol or privilege, and of being engulfed by a wholly intuitive constellation, a seismic and unconscious dimension, the nightsky of a culture that invokes the spectre of dead Gowrie as nightmare protuberance, pregnant hate, "sent dead" against the living to draw blood.

Thus begins a rare pressure of mental imagery within the contours of factual deed, a subtle fable of mental exactitude, therapeutic dimension: rare pressure because it is an alliance or link, an immaterial bond, that begins to grow between black Lucas and the youth Charles Mallison from the day Charles experiences the vertigo of stasis. It embodies the art of the *hungan* to unravel the sorcery of hate.

It is the life of complex projection from culture to culture that helps us to read the action of an insensible community in new dark lights. Culture is deed, instantaneous bright deed, as well as active reflection in the depths of otherness. The nature of that reflection is sometimes akin to darkness, sometimes akin to the nightsky, the dark night which alone mirrors constellations and stars invisible in day.

The opening of Vinson Gowrie's grave in sacred Beat Four territory by Charles, Aleck and old Miss Habersham lies at the heart of *Intruder in the Dust*, to establish that the bullet that killed Gowrie did not come from Lucas's gun. That opened grave is prime corollary to young Mallison's physical/psychical fall and is fraught with unsuspected self-discovery that ignites a trajectory which affects the entire community, and discloses internal corruption and treachery within the dignified *persona* of the Gowrie clan. The very spectre of involuntary Voodoo vengeance, sent against an alleged murderer, proves itself in that theatre of a grave as less a matter of inflamed desire for justice by outraged propriety (harsh and sinister rocket from a fortress of strength) and more a symptom of internal disease within hoary tradition itself. The excavation is done at night and is a prime corollary to young Mallison's fall, less into night as calendrical spirit and more into eclipsed heterogeneity and exactitude of conscience, eclipsed indebtedness of partial systems to partial systems.

The effect is seismic within the narrative bodies of *Intruder in the Dust*. But beneath all convolution and upheaval, it is the mental imagery, the active conscience, that continues to haunt us within and beyond the Voodoo category of harlequin dead. For that mental imagery, or translated spectre of the dead-in-the-living, raises the myth of assessing the *exact shape of spirit*, the weight of spiritual conscience, to rouse itself from the sleep of material habit or age. And one finds one has entered the ground of myth. The shape of conscience is live myth, measureless foundations within daylight premises of buried cultures. Its weight torments us with a sensation of acute impartiality and hope that flits before us within diseased power-structures. That acuteness, or vision of impartiality and hope, ignites an obsession with exact force that, however, remains immeasurable. It flits before us within man-made and nature-made terrors and structured misconceptions. It reveals an appetite in entrenched insensible community to inflict damnation upon others and upon itself.

All this pushes us to reflect upon the action of image, or the dynamism of metaphor, the "alchemy of the word" as the French poet Arthur Rimbaud put it. In my judgement, we tend to confuse spiritual exactitude with static particularity and this breeds narrative-reflections of deeds and objects that are passive in the mind's eye. But mental imagery—as it is beginning to disclose itself to us—is much more than that, it is the activity of live myth, it is much less an appeal to a passivity of mind than a bridge, however precarious, between day-life (or deed-life) and night-life (or indebtedness of bright partial suns to darkest genesis of stars).

The Shadow of Conscience

Even before young Mallison, Aleck Sander and elderly Miss Habersham set out to stay the hand of the lynch-mob by opening Vinson Gowrie's grave, the shadow of excavated premises falls over the region. It is a shadow that lays bare the land as another "spectral carcass" deeded by generation to generation, "cryptic three-toed prints . . . like a terrain in miniature out of the age of the great lizards." The shadow envelops Charles in the theatre of creek and reflected grave—his clothing becomes soft, leaden—as he emerges that cold winter morning to become the unwilling recipient of Lucas's commanding hospitality. He, Aleck Sander and Edmonds' boy are led by Lucas into the shadow that falls everywhere. It drapes the gate through which they pass into Lucas's territory.[5]

The accent upon fossil terrain is part and parcel of the grave of history and of shadow that lays bare the land. All this is underlined by an accumulation and ramification of images within the very cabin in which Lucas lives where Charles confronts a "framed "portrait -group" in which Molly, Lucas's wife, appears like "an embalmed corpse through the hermetic glass lid of a coffin."[6]

The sensation of a sarcophagus—which one cannot fail to experience—possesses a significance that needs to be scrutinised. For one learns later in the novel that Molly and elderly Miss Habersham had grown up like twins. They had both been suckled at Molly's mother's breast. Molly was the daughter of one of Miss Habersham's grandfather's slaves. The two children had slept in the same room, the white girl in a bed, Molly in a cot at the foot of that bed. When Molly and Lucas had their first child Miss Habersham had stood up "in the Negro Church" as godmother.[7]

One is under little or no illusion about the gulf between Miss Habersham and Molly. Despite Miss Habersham's godmother status, they have already moved into separate ghettos. Thus the conception of white and black twins is static attire and Molly's "embalmed corpse" becomes a device to endorse that static dress and to suggest intuitively the dead-end of a cultural homogeneous model.

There is another aspect to Molly's "embalmed corpse." I find that it mimics and brilliantly parodies events to come, in particular the double-headed coffin of Vinson Gowrie, in which one Jake Montgomery is also buried, as Charles Mallison, Aleck Sander and Miss Habersham discover when they open Vinson Gowrie's grave.

Despite such ramifications in the imagery of the novel that expose the dead-end reign of a corrupt regime—however dignified it appears on the surface in its daylight epitaphs and deeds—Faulkner (through Lawyer Stevens, Charles's uncle) devotes long passages to defend territorial-in-moral imperative. Herein lies his instructive failure to perceive the heterogeneous potential and cross-cultural mind within the shadow of *Intruder in the Dust*, so that that potential twinship—so remarkably manifest in creative intuition—freezes and aborts itself until it even seduces the intellect to erect a passive inverted twin pawn in the game of power politics. The very tone, the very voice of Lawyer Stevens's barren intellectuality, implies "Faulkner's assumption," as Edmond L. Volpe puts it, "of the role of spokesman for the South."

Lucas is reduced, in Lawyer Stevens's argument, to an inverted pawn in North/South politics of culture. The "privilege of setting him free" rests with territorial factor or ruling majority in Faulkner's South and cancels out original mentality or initiative, not only between the outside world (symbolised by the North) and the inside world (symbolised by the South), but also between blacks and whites since it rests with the collective whites alone—within a game of *imposed* unity—to set "Sambo free."[8]

The unity of the intuitive self (as darkened psychical pool of concentration) and its capacity to undermine the logic of ego-historical bias or one-sided moral imperative is an issue of unconscious irony, which is implicit in our exploration. Indeed, that realm of unconscious irony helps to redeem Faulkner's lapses and to give to Lawyer Stevens's homilies a sense of automatic carnival. For Faulkner and Lawyer Stevens are involuntary twins, both passive and active in turn. They are less absolute author (Faulkner) and fictional subject (Stevens), and more an automatic catalyst to invoke a series of ambiguous twinships in a mosaic self-portrait; namely, Molly and Miss Habersham (who share the same static cradle), Vinson Gowrie and Jake Montgomery (who in turn share the same coffin), Vinson Gowrie's twin brothers who share

the same puppet-like destiny, and other insensible twins within
theatre of the grave and cradle that tends to parody itself unwittingly and involuntarily.

In the context of carnival or masked comedy and upheaval which
disperses reflections of form (reflections on the mutability rather
than immutability of character) we may perceive, I think, the
fascinations of *shared ego or desire for conquest* entrenched within
cultures. This brings home the reality of evil, in which cultures are
enmeshed in codes to invert or overturn each other rather than
become involved in complex mutuality and the difficult creation of
community.

Inverted pawns in the game of civilisation may cloak themselves
in refined or stoical patterns of behaviour, or classical comedy of
manners, which masquerades as order. They may accept a
hierarchy of structures. Treaties are signed between those above
and those beneath. Protocol is established. All seems well. And yet
in broad daylight, as it were, the shadow of conscience drapes itself
everywhere to become a different bridge, a potential bridge, across
a dangerous divide.

TWO

The Schizophrenic Sea

Carnival Twinships

Faulkner's difficulty in relinquishing a conviction of territorial conscription of moral imperative, and the implicit polarisations such order engenders between outsiders and insiders, minority and majority cultures—with one side or the other arrogating to itself the determination of rights or principles—has its roots in legacies of conquest and in tormented monoliths of the nineteenth and twentieth centuries.

One of the first major tormented monoliths to appear in American fiction is *Arthur Gordon Pym of Nantucket.*[1] This was first published in the late 1830s and has since become a peculiar classic. The schizophrenic genius of Edgar Allan Poe in this strange narrative helps us to begin to perceive the decay of order conditioned by conquest; that order begins to review its daylight deeds, made sacrosanct by institutional codes, in the night-time rebellious dream life of the half-conscious and unconscious psyche.

Subversive review however was not Poe's intention, which was instead committed to an ego-conviction of necessary robot-deity or divine slave-master, commander of ships, commander of families, in nineteenth-century America. In *Pym*, versions, and inversions, of divine commander are mirrored in Captain Block and in other figures on land and sea as well as in black and white mutineers and rebels.

It seems to me an illuminating perspective of unconscious irony in *Intruder in the Dust* to move Faulkner's Lucas Beauchamp backward into Poe's schizophrenic high seas and place him within a previous incarnation as the authoritarian black mutineer Seymour who sails on Pym's carnival ship *Grampus*.

It is a comparison that may seem extreme at first sight, since Faulkner's Lucas is possessed by the appearances of unswerving dignity, whereas Poe's Seymour is painted as an executioner and fiend in a world fired by hate. Extreme as it is, it reveals a pathology of emotions in two classic American novels, a state of emotion governed by projections of fear across the generations from which may be minted bizarre currencies of the imagination that suffer violence or erupt into violence.

Lucas Beauchamp reflects an iron pride, a pitiless comedy of manners, a capacity to suffer insult and remain unbowed, a conviction of fanatical uprightness and superiority in the twentieth century that outrages Faulkner's whites for whom pride and superiority are commodities of tradition reserved to themselves.

Seymour reflects an authoritarian conviction in the nineteenth century, a pitiless capacity to inflict injury upon oppressor and oppressed who stand in his way. This alarms Poe's masochistic creativity, since he himself is torn between the state of tyranny, as material of the divine to be challenged, and the dream of rebellion, as gross sin to be punished. Seymour appals as judge and executioner rolled into one agent of authoritarian rebel in divine slave-master on Poe's sailing ship *Grampus* in the wake of mutiny.

Lucas inspires dread because he dons the Faulknerian mask of the victim who gauges nevertheless, with cunning insight, the vulnerable proportions of lynch-mob or lynch-god. That that lynch-god wears a white collective mask and possesses many hands only heightens the nemesis of black-masked Seymour who lusts for power and of inverted pawn Lucas who attires himself in the stoical attributes of the *status quo*.

This equation between Seymour, the authoritarian Poesque rebel, and nihilist, pitiless authority—an equation of pervasive irony in twentieth-century global politics, in inverted Latin American and Third World cultures which have wrested freedom from brutal empires they still emulate—is a measure of doomed symmetry or the death of the very freedom that appears to have been won.

Instead of freedom, doom presides; it resides in the acceptance of absolute structure within partial institutions that have
masqueraded for centuries as the divine parentage of the modern
world.

On the other hand, the complex breaches of partial, yet schizo-
phrenically closed, order or symmetrical religious fate (by which
Poe was haunted in his time) suggest that, in our time, there may
exist another reading of events within the womb of cultural space; a
reading that perceives meaningful distortions planted by the
intuitive self within a work of the imagination—such as *Pym*—that
symbolises ambiguities of freedom—distortions that disclose
varieties of *unstructured vision or unconscious arbitration* that me-
diate between all structured systems, all masks or deeds within
that work.

Such mediation, I believe, is the irony of forces within the
intuitive self—the irony of changed and changing emotions within
the address of art—one discovers but cannot entrap. That address
releases unsuspected potential, or mutated fabric, to absorb the
stresses of genuine change within obsolescent order and to warn
against every beguilement to succumb to age-old parody of
imperial family or divine state, and to repetitive cycles of violence.

I should perhaps elaborate on the play of unstructured vision
or arbitrating forces secreted in the indirections/directions,
tendencies/upheavals, *within* and *through* partial systems, though
I hope that the variables of this conception will emerge in our
explorations as insight into alchemy of image and word rather than
as intellectual statement.

The play of arbitrating forces should be associated with an
asymmetry within the infinity and genius of art. This does not in
any way imply that symmetries are false but it demonstrates that
orders of symmetry may appear universal—may seek to pre-empt
infinity—though they may actually be no more than useful,
sometimes brilliant, extensions and inversions of a binding
prejudice and locality. The stranger beauty of asymmetry lies in its
subtle transformations of phenomena bound or tamed within a
mask of universality and within patterns of elegant
tautology—sometimes within patterns of unconscious parody of
the past—sometimes within patterns that seek to reify territorial
legend into moral or conquistadorial imperative symmetrised by
habit or education into our perception of humanity.

Symmetries may be disrupted meaningfully, therefore, by the pressure of intuitive and subtle infinity upon localities of hubris masquerading as universal, an infinity of pressure whose truth ultimately resists every cage, to offer itself instead in the complex interactions of partial images as these disclose themselves subject to untamed and untamable resources within, yet beyond, daylight capture or framework.

Untamed and untamable infinity is a temptation to paranoia and it places undeniable stress on human sensibility, but its gifts to the human imagination, its corollaries of ongoing and ceaselessly unfinished explorations in the arts and sciences, are rewarding beyond measure. It confirms the necessity for complex mutuality between cultures. It offers, in my judgement, the only doorway into a conception of genuine breakthrough from tragedy. It has become a cliché to speak of the death of tragedy, but the growth of nihilism, the growth of ideologies that make pawns of humanity, the end-of-the-world syndrome in which we live, would all seem to be motivated by stoic lust or conviction, stoic intellectuality, the inverse nobility of tragedy.

Tragedy lives, and within our carnival age it implies a passivity that accepts the fate of catastrophe with little or no genuine complaint, it accepts the ultimate inversion of all by a structured and tamed nature that becomes, in stages, a decadent and fatally diseased or exploited muse. Carnival tragedy stresses, therefore, ultimatum or the hollow mask humanity wears with a semblance of dignity.

Asymmetric infinity, on the other hand, implies an enfolding and unfolding of cultures beyond tamed vision, or totalitarian caprice and loss of revolutionary soul, it implies unseen yet real natures whose life is indefatigable (and thus it may, indeed must, occasion a sense of exhaustion within ephemeral structuralism), and whose therapeutic horizons-in-depth lie beyond logical fate that frames canvases of existence.

These distinctions may, I hope, prove helpful at this stage though much more needs to be said on the mystery of injustice and mental pain, and whether the innocent may not suffer at times less from tragic fate and more from a lust for symmetry, by underpinning localities of hubris to polarise cultures into 'universal' camps that have no alternative but to articulate the death of others (and implicitly, in a nuclear age, of mankind) by inversions of blood and pitiless codes and fractions of violence in the response of one universal hierarchy to another. Herein lies the abnormal tension of Poe's *Pym* and the corruption of violence it portrays, a corruption in addiction to the death of mankind Poe constructs with realistic fa'lacy on his schizophrenic high seas.

Poe's fear of alien appearances—his subjection to the charisma of *blackness* and *whiteness*—helps us to see that his animus against the 'black person' or 'black enemy' was an obsessional neurosis that disabled him in the exercise of the very authority of freedom he idolised. Yet it gave him a singular concentration upon extreme or tormenting faculties by which he was conscripted. Sidney Kaplan writes in his introduction to *The Narrative of Arthur Gordon Pym*, "Poe, who has seemed to many an anguished man set apart from his times, was, in fact, a part of the American Nightmare. In the decade of the founding of Garrison's *Liberator*, of Nat Turner's conspiracy, of Theodore Weld's *The Bible Against Slavery*, he felt called upon to say that slavemasters violated no law divine."[2]

Poe's defence of the institution of slavery in nineteenth-century America is an intellectual paradox. It was an attitude that may have been cemented by emotional and ambivalent memories. Some biographers speak of his ambivalence toward his foster-father, admiration at one stage, loathing at another, and something akin to symbolic mutiny comes through in *Pym* in the organs of family and state against which Pym and his companions mutiny to incur a burden of guilt, manifesting a greed to be punished for having sinned against surrogate divinity.

The masks surrogates wear in *Pym* are the substance of carnival twinships, carnival tragedy that gleams with asymmetric fissures of myth. We need to be clear, I think, about the strength of hollow ultimatum or mask in *Pym* which slips from the brow of character to character like the highwater mark of nihilistic tragedy even as it borders upon untamed potential for re-birth in the womb of space.

There is Captain Block's 'ultimatum' which would have left Pym to drown at sea. There is Pym's grandfather who threatens to cut his grandson off without a shilling and who comes close to assaulting him. There is the black mutineer Seymour on the *Grampus* on whom Poe projects his fears of authoritarian rule and repression.[3] These are a few prime examples of ultimatum that overshadows Pym.

Intriguing fissures in the Block ultimatum reflect unnamable mediation at the helm of the cosmos arbitrating between the 'death of the land' (a phrase that may help to illumine the density of Pym's emotion of decaying and claustrophobic family regime) and the 'womb of the sea.' That this intuition does flourish for a moment is demonstrated in the re-birth of Pym and Augustus from the paradoxical and cruel sea in the wake of their rebellion against the land—against the institutional corpses of family and state—a rebellion that is augmented by the only successful mutiny throughout the entire narrative of *Pym*, when the crew of Block's ship disobey his orders not to search for survivors from the *Ariel* but are harmoniously wedded to him again in restoring Pym and Augustus to life. It is an intuition that is imperilled. Block and his surrogates are conscripted afresh into a chain of authoritarian mutineers and hollow commanders of the globe.

Tragic crew of the globe—masked by re-born (yet aborted) Augustus and Pym—succumb to greed or guilt to punish themselves within a repetitive cycle of blocks to freedom. The miraculous re-birth from the womb of the sea is fatally tainted, or rendered abortive, it seems, by the very mutinies that occasion it. Fatally tainted mask, yet miraculous fissure or arbitrating insight, remains in each bleak step from twinship to twinship.

The first twinship *Ariel* within a series of psychical or dream-association is overturned by Captain Block, and Pym and Augustus are rescued by Block's mutineers to escape drowning by the skin of their teeth. Thus they become psychical twins and undergo a "partial interchange of character."[4] It is a nightmare excursion, akin to overwhelming dream; it is a medium of re-birth paradoxically sprung, in the first place, from their disobedience and the deception they practised on their parents. The dream sea from which they are rescued registers the taint of original disobedience by painting its highwater mark of insensibility upon Augustus's brow, carnival block, as it were.

It is he who had encouraged Pym, in a drunken fit, to trick their parents, steal out of their homes, and set sail at midnight on the *Ariel*. Pym discovers too late that Augustus "had drunk far more than I suspected, and . . . his conduct . . . had been the result of a highly concentrated state of intoxication . . . which, like madness, enables the victim to imitate the outward demeanour of one in perfect possession of his senses. . . . He was now thoroughly insensible" as he held the tiller of the dream-ship *Ariel*.[5]

Thus it is that Augustus, though re-born twin to Pym from the womb of the sea, had previously, incorrigibly, slipped into 'block insensibility' to echo and mirror (to parody unwittingly) past and future blanket of indifference that Captain Block himself casts over the sea when the *Ariel* is overturned and Augustus and Pym are all but drowned. It is as if ruling Captain Block and insensible victim Augustus, at the helm of the overturned *Ariel*, share a mutual incorrigibility and projection of hollowness from one to the other.

The psychical re-birth/twinship between Augustus and Pym is established within ruling 'block insensibility', as it were. Asymmetric fissure of hope glimmeringly and intuitively exists but the wound of guilt is pathological and severe, and it begins to fester into recurring mutiny and authoritarian malaise.

If the *Ariel* is the first twinship, then the second—in interwoven physical stage and psychical insight—occurs on the *Grampus*. Here the head of block—with its ingrained wound—is worn by both Pym's white grandfather and the authoritarian mutineer Seymour whose existence we have already tentatively outlined as nineteenth century incarnation of Faulkner's twentieth century Lucas Beauchamp. The notion that Pym's white grandfather is psychical twin to black Seymour is scarcely Poe's conscious intention. He achieves it unknowingly through "partial interchange[s] of character" and carnival usage of pigmentations. Through one mask he lays bare the shadowy gestures or omens concealed in another.

A certain decorum is adopted in depicting Pym's harsh grandfather who raises his umbrella against Pym as if it were a weapon when Pym is on his way to embark surreptitiously on the *Grampus*. No such restraint is necessary in painting Seymour with an axe in his hand on the deck of the *Grampus* in the wake of mutiny.[6]

It is on the *Grampus* that Block's metaphysical, terrifying and shifting mask possesses Augustus again. He becomes Pym's involuntary tormentor and gaoler. As with the *Ariel*, he had played a decisive hand in outwitting Pym's parents and concealing Pym in the hold of the ship. There Pym suffers the torments of the damned to which Augustus is insensible. Mutiny has broken out three days after the *Grampus* sailed and Augustus has no alternative but to abandon Pym to a fate that resembles drowning at sea within the black hold of a slave ship.

Pym surfaces again after his dreadful incarceration and Augustus is the one who begins to descend into gangrenous darkness of soul as the mutiny breaks into warring factions and the *Grampus* is stricken by pitiless elements.

Augustus's mask of psychical twinship in Pym's affections is slowly absorbed into the features of Dirk Peters, a stalwart mutineer on the *Grampus*. We need to pay close attention, I would suggest, to the depth of this conversion in the context of the carnival ambivalences we have been exploring. For one is now in a position to perceive in the novel *Pym* a profound and irrational coherence uncannily close to pre-Columbian or ancient American masquerade or myth that arcs or runs from North through Central into South America. Note that Dirk Peters is of Amerindian stock, that his antecedents are pre-Columbian. Let us also note some essential and clearly visible motifs of masquerade in which inversions and replacements, transfusions of psychical blood occur.

Just as Pym and Augustus share psychical blood after the collision between the *Ariel* and Captain Block's ship, Amerindian Peters and black Seymour are psychically twinned in the act of bloody mutiny on the *Grampus*. Augustus dies in the midst of the torments the mutineers suffer. So does Seymour. Augustus is swallowed within an ultimatum that aborts his twinship to Pym. Seymour is possessed by the corpse of the land when he succumbs to a ruse Pym's faction plays on him. Pym leads the assault by masquerading as the galvanized corpse of a dead seaman, galvanized institution of decaying family or state.

The victorious faction led by Pym appears to have no alternative in the ensuing weeks but to resort to cannibalism and consume the sole survivor from Seymour's party. This is the climax of hideous proportions foreshadowed in the consumption by fate of both Seymour and Augustus. Cannibalism is foreshadowed by psychical stomach and devouring insight into a dying age whose fate leaves every survivor a metaphysical orphan, metaphysical blood to be consumed or to be re-born.

The eclipse of Augustus leaves Pym brotherless and orphaned. The fall of Seymour leaves Peters also bereft. Thus it seems natural that Pym and Peters resume the thread of precarious hope, precarious motif of true relationship in re-birth, left vacant or twisted in the deaths of Augustus and Seymour.

However natural it seems, Peters is the most unprepossessing twin Pym could have adopted or found. Pym makes this abundantly clear in the repulsion he expresses on first meeting Peters. Peters is "one of the most purely ferocious-looking men I ever beheld. . . . His hands, especially, were so enormously thick and broad as hardly to retain a human shape. . . . His head was equally deformed, being of immense size, with an identation on the crown (like that on the head of most Negroes), and entirely bald."[7]

It is a vision that makes fissured sense only when read in the context of enthralling weight exercised by the block phenomenon to which Pym belongs. The apparent ugliness of Peters is a measure of Pym's fascination with varieties of carnival pigment in a cruel age. Just as the ferocity of Seymour exposes the violence masked by decorum in Pym's grandfather, so Peters's hideousness dramatises Pym's addiction to an age he is unable to expose except by projecting his great fear of it into apparently alien pigmentations and features. Peter's features, therefore, are less a realistic portrait than a fissure or crack into deep-seated ambivalences in Pym himself.

In the course of the ensuing narrative, that projection upon Peters is gradually withdrawn to come home in galvanized corpses that rear their heads upon Pym himself (when he masquerades as one in a fearful scene on the ship). They rear their heads also upon a mysterious passing vessel manned by dead men that seem outrageously alive with the motion of the vessel as it approaches and passes the *Grampus*.[8]

That nameless vessel may well be perceived as a third twinship in the series commencing with the *Ariel*. If so, the fourth is the *Jane Guy*, which comes upon the wrecked *Grampus* drifting at sea, and saves the lives of 're-born twins' Pym and Peters. It is a fascinating unconscious irony that after the *Jane Guy* itself is gutted and destroyed in the Antarctic by metaphysical blacks (their very teeth are black), Pym records—on escaping with Peters—that he and Peters "are the only living *white men* upon the island [italics mine]."[9]

The enthralling yet hideous charm exercised by diseased order upon Pym seems no longer to be projected upon Amerindian Peters. Nevertheless that projection still complexly exists in the white-masked visage black Peters now wears as one perceives the classic Freudian slip Poe brings into the narrative of *Pym* some twenty years or so before the birth of Freud in 1856.

Masquerade and Myth

I spoke earlier of a pre-Columbian bridge of myth that runs through the Americas and with which *Pym* achieves uncanny, however unconscious, synchronicity in the womb of cultural space.

For the purposes of this exploration we may approach the bridge where it is identified with a rainbow arc across Mexico into the Caribbean and Guianas. The masquerading figure associated with the Caribbean and Guianas is Yurokon.[10] He is the fourth in a series of masquerading 'block' gods (twinships of space, in my estimation) upon and beneath that rainbow arc. The first is Quetzalcoatl (bird and snake mask) followed by Kukulcan and Huracan (both of which sustain species of twins of heaven and earth). These mutate into, or are succeeded by, Yurokon (as Roth's inventory of masquerading features suggests) where the bridge arches into the Caribbean and moves into South America.[11]

One of the prime aspects of Yurokon is the blend he achieves between cannibalism and the bone-flute extracted from each victim from whose body a morsel is consumed.[12] By and large, scholars tend to repudiate the burden of ferocity projected onto the Caribs (with whom Yurokon is associated) by the Spanish conquistadores.

"In the sixteenth century," Michael Swan declares in *The Marches of El Dorado*, "the Spaniards excused their enslavement of the island Indians by convincing Europe that anthropophagy was the common custom there. . . . The royal edict gave the colonizers liberty to do as they pleased with Indians who, without any doubt, were not cannibalistic." Swan quotes Richard Schomburgk's *Travels* of the nineteenth century in respect to the Caribs (as distinct from other Indian peoples) who—Schomburgk declared —practised a form of ritual cannibalism and "usually brought back to the settlement an arm or leg of the slaughtered enemy as a trophy, which would then be cooked so as to get the flesh more easily off the bone; a flute was made out of this." In the light of oral traditions and of significant and varied parallels between Yurokon and the origins of Carib cannibalism in Ruth's researches into the animism of the Indians, Swan has no alternative but to state that "the object of (Carib) cannibalism was a kind of transubstantiation in reverse: the bone (flute) contains the living spirit of the dead. . . . ')It was the source of) prophecy and witch-craft . . . (and) transference of spirit."[13]

The bone-flute was a confessional organ involved in, yet subtly repudiating, the evil bias of conquest that afflicted humanity. It sought to invoke an apparition of re-birth clothed in colour and music, the rainbow colour and music of forests, skies and earth in various twinships associated with vegetation and constellation however imperilled these had been by brute appetite for war.

Yurokon's twinship of sea and sky, vegetation and star, was an affirmation of elusive foundations and partial institutions, and of a successive body of dying ages inhabited by precarious organ or bone-flute of re-birth, so subtle it bred a fissure in appearances one tended still to take for granted as absolute or total until they became carnival masks addicted to hubris. As such they could accumulate into an illusion of absolute and fearful command unless they yielded a profound distinction or arbitration between tragedy (as ultimate block) and therapy (as fissure of re-birth into unknown futures to be ceaselessly created though they exist paradoxically in the heights and the depths of eclipsed present and past).

The emergence of asymmetric future through fissured past and present symmetries or models leads to the notion of a bridge that inevitably breaks to convey the paradox of creation in both the heights (above the bridge) and the depths (beneath the bridge).

The descent of a masquerading block, such as Quetzalcoatl of Mexico, into the womb of the sea (that descent is also characteristic of cannibal Carib Yurokon) sustains the *Ariel* motif of potential re-birth (explored in Poe's *Pym*) in contradistinction to insensible or hollow lucidity within static, block commanders who cling to ship or broken bridge, resist descent and become mere spectators of events within the stream or sea or forest of creation beneath them.

The necessity for cannibalism in profound masquerade and myth touches deeply, I believe, upon the anguish of nihilist tragedy. There was no realistic necessity, for example, for the cannibalism practised by Poe's mutineers. Food and drink were available and were salvaged from an area of the *Grampus* immediately after the cannibal feast. This leads one to perceive a psychical and compulsive drama in which Poe was involved despite the apparent factual fallacies with which he justifies excesses of conduct or appearance.

Writers Roth, Schomburgk and Swan approach Yurokon cannibalism as the magic of animism, the acquisition of hidden and secret knowledge from the mind of enemy or deceiving friend. A ritual morsel from the body of enemy or too secretive friend is consumed. A bone extracted from that body becomes the seed of musical spirit, or voice of insight. This leads one to reflect deeply upon the inarticulate dimension of cannibal ritual implicit in the Yurokon myth. It is the fierce suppressed dialogue between *partial* orders masquerading as totalities or absolutes or captain blocks—the tone of terrifying duality as well between inner and outer being—that is at the heart of savage music in all ages, the birth of savage music in polarised cultures, the savage bone-flute. As an age polarises, the stress upon eclipsed dialogue becomes more and more extreme, the necessity to penetrate the other's arsenal of secrets becomes more and more obsessive and compelling. The other, in this context, is both enemy and suspect spy or friend within warring factions at home or abroad. Inevitably as enemy and friend coalesce into deranged order, psychical nemesis or cannibalism is projected upon all persons and creatures. A psychical necessity to consume bias, to relinquish the hubris of conquest, becomes unconscious necessity. Carnival ambiguities and ambivalences arise within the arts, which require an un-ravelling of perspectives and of blocked dialogue between cultures, so that the mystery of freedom may be born and re-born and born again and again within terrifying closure or circumstance that threatens to consume all.

Poe's *Arthur Gordon Pym of Nantucket* is uncannily susceptible to illumination within a medium of pre-Columbian masquerade and myth whose proportions I have outlined. The excesses of Poe's *Pym* begin to yield to judgements and criteria born of the twinship of intuitive self and myth. Although *Pym* is regarded in some quarters as a classic, it remains controversial and is ignored or under-estimated. It may well be a tormented but significant forerunner that bears upon the womb of space in the cross-cultural carnival.

THREE

Concentric Horizons

The Dying God and His Carnival Women

"I am an invisible man. No, I am not a spook like those who haunted Edgar Allan Poe . . ." is the declaration Ellison's protagonist makes at the beginnng of a complex confessional narrative.[1]

It is an important double-edged statement. It cuts, on one edge, into Poe's realistic fallacies and into the hideous portraiture of black men Poe heaps up in *Pym* that tends to conceal the depths of mutuality it sustains with white-masked visage; and on the other edge, invisible man's declaration speaks of the inverted pawns of a civilisation in which motifs of re-birth may be stifled in the guilt of diseased orders.

It is the latter edge that fissures Ellison's major novel. *Invisible Man* is less concerned with twinship than with the womb of an age as this is perceived in an epic, dying god associated with the feminine muses of gold, blood, music and their rich evolutionary potential or their tragically debased fertility in psychical and material senses.

Invisible man is a repetitively dying (yet cyclically re-awakening) god who is metaphorically consumed first in the boxing ring phase of the novel, then in the Bledsoe phase, then in the paint factory explosion phase, and in other succeeding Harlem phases in which he is symbolically castrated yet bleakly 'potentialised', rendered metaphysically potent, within the womb of space.

With each metaphorical death, with each phase of reduction to a cannibalised figure, invisible man undergoes a bleak awakening or re-birth in the envelope of his civilisation. He is no Jonah but the civilisation that threatens to swallow him is part biblical sea or whale's belly metamorphosed, in some degree, into a womb of cultural evolutions.

That womb is symbolised by the signal importance of carnival women or muse figures who appear at each phase or cycle in the narrative. The disadvantages or debasements threaded into these muses make each re-birth or awakening that invisible man experiences bleak and terrifying.

Ellison insists on the solidity of invisible man or dying god who is "a man of substance, of flesh and bone." The stricture on cultural blindness bulks large—"when they approach me they see only my surroundings."[2] Nevertheless "invisibility" is also a fissure in the womb of space, a ripple upon uniform premises, a complex metaphor of the imaginative descent of masquerading stone or solid body into a psychical pool on which concentric circles and horizons appear.

The novel is a confessional narrative. It begins at the end of the series of metaphorical deaths invisible man experiences when he descends into a hole or grave lit by electricity to review all that has happened to him over a long odyssey. In another sense, as already suggested, it is as if an alchemised creature or stone falls into biblical, yet electric, diseased whale adorned with political scenarios of memory to send out concentric ripples or horizons upon the inner yet outer sea of space. The stone, because it is solid, vanishes of necessity. Its invisibility is far-reaching irony of concentric capacities in ceaseless, enclosing, yet expanding cycles.

Concentric horizon or cycle one is the boxing ring set in motion by masquerading stone or descending god that secretes itself/himself in a blues well of music, a blues muse, an ancient mother of scarred freedom/unfreedom, dream-music or well of civilisation associated with Louis Armstrong's "underworld of sound."[3] That underworld of sound yields to a well of terror, a well of forbidden sexuality masked by a naked blonde woman/debased white goddess at the boxing ring where music coalesces with the bewilderments of the mother of freedom into a metaphorical death and ambiguity of re-birth.

Concentric horizon two is the Bledsoe well of tainted scholarship in which the boxing ring mentality re-appears within Golden Day epitaph or asylum of the living dead from all professions. In that tainted well invisible man encounters the womb of space constellated in incestuous Trueblood muses and in a surreal extension of the white goddess.

On concentric horizon three, invisible man 'dies' again in an explosive sea of paint and his bleak re-birth may be constellated with Mary Rambo and other shadowy muses of ambiguous Christian and pre-Christian age.

The blend of Homeric, Anancy (African) and Christian imageries is substantial to the womb of evolutionary space that Ellison seeks in dying (awakening) epic god on each horizon or concentric ring that moves us to step forward and backward into the mutated 'stone' of history. In the context of mutated stone, *Invisible Man* intuitively alters block twinships into a medium of potential and *feminine* horizons, carnival women and muses, upon the rainbow bridge between cultures.

It is within the boxing ring phase, on horizon one, that the first trace is established—through debased carnival white goddess and bewildered blues mother—of linkages of Homeric and Anancy traditions. I shall comment later on the ancient blues muse and her response to invisible man's questions in the well of sound. It is the debased white goddess who presides in terror at the boxing ring of history that ushers in the first ruse or trick of Anancy 'death', half electrocuted, half punch-drunk, invisible man and his awakening into himself as clothed in a Cyclopean (Homeric) mask. "A blow to my head . . .sent my right eye popping like a jack-in-the-box. . . ."[4] Thus invisible man, in association with terrified white goddess, foreshadows in himself the enemy who stalks him and whose secrets he prizes and digests with bewilderment, anguish and bitter gestation within the diseased whale of history.

The Cyclopean mask he himself wears in the deadly boxing ring phase is the start of an inner, pre-figurative acquaintance with others in clinical envelope and political theatre whom he will encounter. They too carry the Cyclopean birth-mark. One is a doctor in a hospital who peers menacingly with "a bright third eye that glowed from the centre of his forehead." Another is Brother Jack in Harlem whose eye squints at invisible man with Cyclopean irritation.[5]

What invisible man begins to learn figuratively and painfully, within the cyclical code that he inhabits, is the fascination of helplessness, the proneness to fall back into, with each arousal from, the Cyclopean nightmare that pursues him as much in his own skull, or Anancy skin, as in rituals of entertainment others impose upon him—repulsive arts, exploited sciences, faked renascences.

This bleakest of perceptions is in itself a measure of uncertain awakening from complex paralysis, it occupies the narrative with unspoken intensity that unsettles the shape of territorial imperative meaning, light is dark ground, gold is false ground, declarations of virtue or rightness may prove to be propaganda and the ground of lies. In this ambiguity of real/unreal performance, the prose of the boxing ring cycle fissures and threads the vitality of muses into hidden counterpoint with invisible man's helplessness; it is a vitality, however, that is so darkened and blocked in terror-stricken white goddess, or muse of electric gold, who presides at the ring, and equally terrified mother of freedom, who presides at the well of blues, that what is apparently unsettled is sealed or closed fast afresh.

Invisible man asks blues "Ma" to tell him the secret of freedom but her enraged sons threaten him for making their great and confused mother—great and confused prisoner of history—cry.[6]

However disadvantaged or debased these vital muses are, they still potentialise an imperceptible tide upon which invisible man shape-shifts his helplessness into opposed, yet related, features. He is a black Odysseus in whose fictive, musical blood Anancy runs. His fictive status is a measure of insight into endangered thread of capacity, endangered foetus of freedom in the womb of space.

Ancient Homer tells us that the giant Cyclops Polyphemus would have eaten Odysseus had he not been blinded by the man's cunning. And in this intuitive conjunction of blindness to others (who become hidden, unseen entities) with cannibal Homeric legend (built into feminine horizon), foetal man in Ellison's narrative begins to eat the secret (although he never wholly digests it) of profound and mutual creative responsibility that arches through fathomless sound and sight in mutations of descending stone.

I emphasise the term 'feminine horizon' to make clear that the concentric cycles set in motion by descending man-god—in our reflections upon mutated stone—constitute a shift, not only from carnival twinship to carnival women and muses, but from implicit Poesque cannibal tragedy to implicit Ellisonian cannibal epic. The stress on 'cannibal' is of particular interest in the cross-cultural womb of space; since it links Cyclopean giant to nightmare, it also links foetal hope, or thread of re-born capacity, to Yurokon bone-flute and seed of music explored in the last chapter.

It is true that carnival twinship did imply a womb of sea and space (and that the feminine projection was concealed in the elements) but the shift which is visible in *Invisible Man* is a subtle stroke of genius, and consists in unravelling the masked presence of the female upon or beneath rainbow arcs or bridges between cultures. This, I believe, is fundamental to the secret of a renewal of epic in the twentieth century and it reveals the bleakness of awakenings black Odysseus experiences when the female is consistently disadvantaged. The Bledsoe cycle is particularly instructive in this respect in that it suggests that the gestation of foetal man of history remains unfulfilled because of incestuous muse that comes to reflect hideously tainted memories affecting all relationships invisible man recalls in the urban, electric and diseased whale of civilisation into which he descends to write his confessions. The link between foetal man's nightmare and the Cyclopean giant envelope enclosing him remains unhappily static or dominant and largely unbroken.

Bledsoe/Golden Day and Trueblood Women

The Bledsoe phase in the black Odysseus's bitter epic is marked by Bledsoe's sophisticated tyrannies and lies, and by blind Homer Barbee's rhetoric in preaching of black freedom and black scholarship.[7] But it is darkly true, I find, that the *emotion* of tyranny, and chauvinist scholarship, is rooted less in sophisticated lies and comedy of manners, and more in implicit territory of gestations; a fettered being upon a treadmill in the womb of space. The womb of space is so sealed that the Bledsoe lie becomes as incorrigible as nihilist military heroes, nihilist lawyers, nihilist doctors, nihilist industrialists who inhabit the Golden Day.

The emphasis on layers of gestation that neither abort nor come to birth makes it self-evident that Trueblood territory runs deeper than clichéd sexual structure adorned by theories of frustration or repression. Not that frustration and repression are ignored, they do exist, but as transitive chords, as fissured dimension, into a deeper orchestration or pressure of sealed womb in which invisible man is confined. It is a prison made all the more vivid in the light of insights that take no comfort in escapism or commercial heavens. That the lure of escapism is a hollow dream is the bleakest of awakenings in itself to the formidable, subtle, complex creativity required if genuine epic, genuine community (rather than commodities of faked renascence) is to be recovered in depth.

There is a distinction, in other words, between clichéd sex, clichéd renascence and *coniunctio* or true marriage, true re-birth.

The confinement invisible man endures translates itself, when Bledsoe expels him from haven and college, into inevitable illiteracy of the imagination, into continuity of sealed space, hollow certificates, hollow letters of recommendation carried in the hope they will advance his fame and fortune in the world; they are designed by Bledsoe to invert him into a running pawn. They are witness to an illiteracy of the imagination masked by Machiavellian and academic creed. They bind him all the more frighteningly to an alphabet of nightmare.

The inner alphabet of ecstasy, the hoped-for renascence of epic brotherhood of man, tends to be sealed away again and again, and this issue of tormenting horizon translates itself into various perversions or traumatic deed that comes into broad daylight. A prime illustration in the Bledsoe phase lies in Trueblood's sexual intercourse with his daughter, Matty Lou.[8]

Trueblood wakes, or is awakened by his wife Kate Trueblood, to the intercourse in which he is engaged with Matty Lou Trueblood. Daylight reconnaissance of the deed, in all its shame, pleasure and horror, makes him a monster to some, a hero to others. For example, when he tells his story to unhappy Odysseus (then a student at Bledsoe's college) and to fascinated Norton (a white, Olympian trustee), Norton is transported by confused emotions and recalls the portrait of a lost daughter he had idolised. When the tale is over, Norton seals the pact of vicarious incest that he shares with Trueblood with an economic hand-out. The deed thus acquires an economic sanction.

It possesses also a hidden institutional sanction in that Bledsoe's power over both Olympian Norton and Ellison's Odysseus is written into the conventional rhetoric and morality that subsist on pawns of humanity, within the womb of space, who are the obscure equivalents to an alphabet of ecstasy turned into letters of incest—into economic hand-out, on one hand, to pay for vicarious pleasures and entertainments—into chauvinist scholarship, on the other, to confirm a wilderness of gestating politics, gestating community, that reinforces every Bledsoe regime. "'They picked poor Robin clean,' I said. 'Do you happen to know Bled?'"[9]

How does invisible man imply eclipsed alphabet of ecstasy beneath monster Trueblood and nihilist Olympian Norton? He is susceptible to plucked and stricken numbers, to the clockwork language of fate, into which Trueblood runs. Beneath the voracious spectre of the clock, a surreal timelessness clothes itself in an extension of terrified white goddess whose forbidden sexuality, in the boxing ring phase, now cracks and yields. She infuses Trueblood (as if he is a surrogate mask black Odysseus wears) with her own terror by "grabbing him round the neck" until "a flock of little white geese flies out of the bed."[10] Her guilt and her terror are his. Or is it that his guilt and his terror become hers? They become so large and yet so nimble that he runs frantically like Alice through the looking glass into the clock on the wall of the room and up a dark tunnel. That is the nebulously exact moment, the timeless moment, when he unconsciously embraces and enters Matty Lou, his grown daughter who sleeps in the same bed with him and his wife in the crowded shack in which they live.

One says 'timeless or nebulously exact moment' because the weight of dream-woman and dream-daughter cannot be established in partial reality. They are a joint clock and well of emotion, a sublimated, yet surreal, extension of both ancient blues mother of scarred freedom (metamorphosed into helpless yet consenting Matty Lou) and terrified blonde woman at the boxing ring (metamorphosed into "flying geese") within whom invisible man first gained, and regains, an insight into himself as clothed in Cyclopean monster and mask, Cyclopean trueblood.

The ground of ecstasy—so swiftly turned into incest—lies in a mutuality of contrasting yet embracing presences, complex rainbow arc of mankind as the secret of epic. The seal that

imprisons such mutuality, kills ecstasy and leaves in its train a
blind contract and broken bridge in daylight reconnaissance. The
innocence of "white geese" converts into the clockwork machine of
the sun. The lightning flash of spontaneous flying carnival fails to
bridge the divide in humanity that consolidates into nightmare,
incestuous block, incestuous wealth, incestuous poverty, incestuous family at the heart of day.

Jean Toomer's Anti-climactic Marriage of Dan and Muriel in Box Seat

Jean Toomer's *Cane* (in which *Box Seat* occupies a significant
place) appeared in 1923, a quarter of a century or so before
Invisible Man was published.[11] It possesses an intuitive, almost
prophetic bearing, I believe, upon Ellison's paradoxes of dying
god/masquerading stone. In texture and style, however, it differs
markedly from Ellison's cyclical novel. It is also less epic in thrust
and more stream-of-consciousness, prose-lyric theatre. Its
originality lies in an abrupt, uneven, contract of emotions that
remains anti-climactic and unfulfilled. The stream-of-consciousness
metaphysic that informs its community of character is wholly
unlike the interior flow, or insistent pressure, that envelops
consciousness in James Joyce's *Ulysses*. Much of *Cane*, one
understands, was written before 1923; some of it had appeared
earlier in American magazines, and it is doubtful whether Toomer
was acquainted with Joyce's masterpiece, published in 1921, when
he wrote *Cane*.

Toomer's stream-of-consciousness seems to me profoundly
native to his American psyche; it is an apt disruption of an
ancestral auction block world and of *person* in *property*, *person* as
property. One has a sensation almost of guilty sleight-of-hand that
shakes auction block securities, auction block psychologies, until
formal properties float into masquerading carnival person,
masquerading Christian stone.

A continent sinks down. The new-world Christ will need consummate
skill to walk upon the waters where huge bubbles burst. . . . Thuds of
Muriel coming down. Dan turns to the piano and glances through a stack
of jazz music sheets. . . . [He] feels the pressure of the house, of the rear

room, of the rows of houses, shift to Muriel. He is light. He loves her. He is doubly heavy.[12]

That curious passage, in which new-world Christ walks on water, reflects the miracle of stone, the carnival transubstantiation, that Dan seeks to invoke in reaching out toward his desired bride Muriel, whose "thuds" resist him to make clear her endorsement of an anchorage of security which she feels herself unable to transform, and against which Dan, despite the apocalyptic fascination he exercises upon her, seems but an impractical drifter destined to sink into oblivion.

Muriel is but one of Toomer's elusive 'brides' (sometimes sacred whores) in *Cane* who, in various ways, resist their ineffectual suitors. But Muriel is the most sensitive, most self-conscious, of them all, and she is aware (half-consciously, with almost puppet-like undertones) of Dan's intricate need of her within a creation of revolutionary art that he seeks to wed, an inner theatre he seeks to re-make against the tide of history. She seems to be driven by a sceptical yet sympathic perception of the mask of "new-world Christ" Dan wears; and in response to this adorns herself with gaudy but implicit rainbow attire to match his fantasy. She seeks support from another puppet-like creature, Bernice. On arrival at Lincoln Theatre she "leads Bernice who is a cross between a washerwoman and a blue-blood lady, a washer-blue, a washer-lady. . . . Muriel has on an orange dress. Its colour could clash with the crimson box-draperies, its colour would contradict the sweet rose smile her face is bathed in, should she take her coat off. . . . Pale purple shadows rest on the planes of her cheeks. Deep purple comes from her thick-shocked hair."[13]

The desired, yet never achieved, marriage between Dan and Muriel is a token of a larger and deeper problem that obsesses Toomer. The mixture of perspectives that he pursues in *Box Seat*—theatre, stream-of-consciousness fiction, lyrical presences— is an indication of changed, inner/outer dialogue he seeks. He needs a revisionary splendour beyond conventional props and lies to overthrow a world of illusion that is built on auction block puppetries, puppet illuminations, puppet houses in which flesh and blood remain sealed and rarely afloat, or a psychical miracle of stone in alchemies of space.

Dan's defeat in the theatre, his disappearance into a sea of streets
and houses, at the end of *Box Seat*, becomes a measure of Toomer's
integrity, his despair with sexual puppetry or artistry of lies. Dan's
failed marriage to Muriel becomes a galvanic, rather than mutual,
rose.

The prime substance of that galvanic rose, that failed marriage,
is dramatised with uneven and evocative intensity in the ambiguity
of a dwarf (a surrogate Christ, a leper invisible to all) who kisses
the rose with battered lips and makes it into a sponge of blood. This
is the nebulously exact moment of anti-climactic marriage between
Dan and Muriel. The dwarf appears in the theatre and sings to
Muriel a "high-pitched, sentimental" song, a song that is unable to
voice what it seeks to express. Thus its sentimentality becomes all
the more telling, all the more absurd, yet moving and alarming as
failed element, failed thunder, in the wake of lightning "mirror
flash." The song, fraught with gaudy emotion, comes to an end.
The dwarf bows to Muriel. Then he offers the blood-soaked rose
"first having kissed it. Blood of his battered lips is a vivid stain
upon its petals."[14]

Muriel flinches back, unable to accept. "Hate pops from [the
dwarf's] eyes and crackles like a brittle heat about the box" as if to
confirm the failed thunder of deity. Then the dwarf's tight-skinned,
lightning brow changes, grows calm, profound, "a thing of wisdom
and tenderness."[15] It is as if a path of genuine submission to
Muriel's limited comprehension (or incomprehension) of
revolutionary theatre surfaces, a wise response to her freedom, her
right *not* to accept the galvanic rose, her right also to question its
premises of sudden tenderness and transubstantial capacity; her
right not to be conscripted by a chorus of politics or convention.
But then that chorus violently intervenes to coerce her. "Arms
reach out, grab Muriel. . . . Claps are steel fingers that manacle
her wrists and move them forward to acceptance." Muriel, "tight in
her revulsion, sees black" but has no alternative but to accept the
gift of battered lips upon the rose and to grow blind to the mystery
of the transformed brow of wisdom she may have begun to
glimpse.

It is then that Dan's despair explodes. He springs up and shouts,
"Jesus was once a leper." It is a half-mad declaration, a regression
into galvanic lips, mask of hate, the dwarf has shed but he appears
to resume. He steps down, "cool as a green stem that has just shed

its flower," yet remains in regressed circumstance in league with bloodstained sponge in the dwarf's outstretched hand. The green stem begins to vanish into the soil of the theatre, anti-climactic theatre.[16]

As he moves toward the exit and confronts the schizophrenic rage in himself and in the violent chorus or audience around him, his memory darkens still further and descends within the shackled sponge/rose in Muriel and himself, within leper or inverted Ascension of Christ.

His descent is as much a sombre judgement of himself as of others, it is an awkward repudiation of props of violence by which the consummation of mutual blood, mutual being, was defeated at the very moment it may have begun to encompass the rights of otherness as integral to arts of dialogue and truth.

There is an intriguing aspect to *Box Seat* I would like to mention. It is the aspect of parable, biblical parable, which subsists on secret understandings, grounded in hard-won freedoms, rather than coercive politics inevitably grounded in sophistications of violence and the rule of numbers. Toomer may have despaired of an art built on popular models of brute force, and attempted to explore secret signals for those initiated into parables of self-judgement, abruptly changing even irrational signals; for example, hate into tenderness, "new-world Christ" into "Jesus the leper," warm-hearted although sceptical Muriel into blind, insensible muse who accepts the death of the rose in fantasy dwarf or surrogate bridegroom.

All this sustains Toomer's uncompromising rejection of art as an artistic lie masquerading as form, art as fascist privilege or obscene imperative. There is no short-cut, he implies, to alchemical *coniunctio* or true and productive union between man and woman, between one and other, between culture and culture. There is need for complex realities of changed form, revolving and evolving sensibilities. And as such *Box Seat* deepens its proportions of parable into an acceptance in itself of the failure of unhealthy, gaudy sentimentality, a failure that is also an indictment of mass-media nihilist theatre. There is a leprosy to the arts that is unperceived by a conditioned society, Toomer implies, and that leprotic gaiety unconsciously desires relief, unconsciously desires a sacrament of truth.

Box Seat is an American parable and one of the most remarkable confessional short novels associated with the so-called Harlem renaissance. I am tempted to say there is a Kafkaesque nightmare quality to it, though Toomer's sensuous floating images are unlike Kafka's studied, almost clinical envelopes of despair. Some of Kafka's work was published in Europe in his lifetime but nothing, as far as I am aware, had yet been translated into English. Kafka died in 1924 and it is unlikely that Toomer would have heard of him in 1923 when *Cane* was published.

FOUR
The Untamable Cosmos

Structure and Caprice

The last chapter reflected upon 'illiteracy of the imagination' that could rest its hopes on the sealed letters invisible man had been given by Bledsoe to advance his fame and fortune. No such advance was intended by Machiavellian Bledsoe. To the degree that invisible man trusted Bledsoe, he witnessed to an inner helplessness and incapacity to rid himself of the other's corruption. There is a corollary to this, an exposure of ironic narcissim, in a warning Robert Stepto advances in his assessments of Afro-American narrative.[1]

Stepto makes a telling and instructive parallel between articles to which invisible man is obsessively attached when he descends into Harlem and Frederic Douglass's 1845 *Narrative* which "tells us that, in 1835, Douglass and a few of his fellow slaves concocted an escape plan that depended mainly upon each slave's possessing a 'protection' or 'pass', allegedly written by 'Master' William Hamilton but actually composed by Douglass himself. Such a pass granted each man 'full liberty' to travel to Baltimore and spend the Easter holidays. . . . Unfortunately, the plan is thwarted, and each slave has to save his skin by 'denying everything' and destroying his 'forged' protection."[2]

The articles invisible man carries, in addition to the sealed letters, are a leg iron once worn by a slave, a "grinning darky" stereotyped money bank, a Sambo doll, dark glasses, and so on. They, unlike the letters Bledsoe had composed for the eyes only of cynical industrialists who were advised to deceive invisible man with promises they could not fulfil, constitute "passes" into brotherhood, religion and protest politics. By painful degrees, invisible man perceives that the betrayal by black Dr Bledsoe is a twentieth-century, unconscious dramatisation of past humiliations both Bledsoe and his antecedents had endured, and this capacity for dramatic visualisation of sealed word and silent object constitutes the first faint fissure in 'illiteracy of the imagination', the first thread of the conversion of endemic deprivation through and beyond protest politics and soapbox speeches into parables of self-judgement and into abrupt alteration of narcissistic codes. Such bitter thread of truth is the shadow of health in the wake of diseased illiteracy of the imagination that feeds upon propaganda and hollow violence.

The theme of the conversion or the convertibility of unhealthy states into therapeutic parable is implicit to some degree in Robert Stepto's chapter on *Invisible Man* in his study of Afro-American narrative, and in the epigraph to that chapter he quotes from Jay Wright's *Dimensions of History:* "I went to bed sick. I woke up well." Later in this chapter we shall look somewhat closely at certain facets of Jay Wright's long epic poem, *The Double Invention of Komo*, but first we resume our journey through dimensions of cultural space by reflecting upon the Mexican novel *Pedro Páramo* by Juan Rulfo. Rulfo's novel evokes diseased relationships in the sickness of history as prelude to configurations of implicit therapeutic "egg" in Wright's *Komo*.

Lysander Kemp's translation into English of *Pedro Páramo* appeared in 1959. Selden Rodman reviewed it for the *New York Times Book Review* and wrote that "Rulfo, like the great Mexican painter Orozco, views history as a tragic circus in which evil impresarios betray clowns by making them believe in their own masquerade. It is the world of Hieronymus Bosch and Rouault as well as of Orozco, and among writers, of Poe and Faulkner."[3]

One is reminded of Toomer's dwarf/clown. Dan resembles but is *not* an evil impresario in *Box Seat* in the senses Rodman implies in his review of *Pedro Páramo*. Dan does not betray the dwarf in

Lincoln Theatre. He responds to the dwarf as surrogate riddle of psyche, as interchangeable mask of self-judgement upon failed magican, failed bridegroom. The darkness of soul and of memory he experiences springs not from betrayal of others but from a perception of malaise, in himself and others, rooted in the corruption of violence that thwarts every climax of wisdom and tenderness at the heart of the clown of space.

Selden Rodman's review of *Pedro Páramo* is apparently conclusive, but in a cross-cultural context, and when visualised in a perspective that arches through Toomer's *Box Seat*, it may sustain a backward-flowing asymmetric stream-of-consciousness immersed not only in symbolic betrayal of clowns (who are committed to believe their own masquerade) but in craft of space akin to Toomer's sleight-of-hand in floating properties of fate into a parable of justice and truth.

Let us begin with Juan Preciado, who begins his odyssey into half-spatial, half-solid world in seeking to locate his father Pedro Páramo. "I heard the sound of my footsteps on the fieldstones. . . . I found the house at the bridge . . . and knocked on the door. . . . But my hand just knocked on empty air."[4]

The village or settlement where he knocks, where Juan Preciado was born, flows backward to Juan's death in the past. For his death lies actually in the past, a past that is alive in museum cradles and epitaphs, ruins and rumours. Juan is therefore as much of the past as of the *Ariel* floating present—he is live rumour. He knocks on space as if the echoes of the past both clothe and address him in each sounding pavement, wall, stone. He too is alchemised stone but his solidity is ephemeral. And yet in deepest reflection, there is kinship to Ellison's invisible solid in that rumour is a ripple or cyclic horizon upon space; the mystery of the psyche descends, *insoluble* psyche, to propel far-flung voices into space.

Preciado subsists on vacancies of time and place. He is the superstitious weight of ruined houses and other signals of clothed deprivation. He is a living museum close to caricature as he listens in his grave to the conversations of other grave-dwellers who subsist in the flotation of rumoured events in the mind of fiction.

Paradoxically (in line with insoluble psyche—and this is the novel's achievement) he is not to be identified with disintegrations of personality locked into adamant structure or grave but with elusive, half-daemonic, implicitly divine, energy that floods all things yet leaves them hollow in turn to echo with densities of the conceptions and misconceptions of truth in sound, sight, blindness, deafness.

The devastated and depleted senses Rulfo portrays in *Pedro Páramo* highlight a glimmering, faint, and contrasting density of paradisaical emotion available to the energy of daemonic self-consciousness, when that phenomenal energy (one equates it with human genius) re-traces its steps and perceives the flight of glory, the original blaze of glory, in each blackened or burnt or ravaged, tenanted hollow it now sees.

The borderline between tenants of hell and tenants of heaven is as subtle and deceiving as that between the genius of a civilisation (in its profoundly visionary and therapeutic aspects) and the fertile madness and devilishly clever instrumentalities of war that ape that genius. Eternal hell-fire and damnation ape atomic insight and nuclear energy (with resources to transform ritual polarisations and alleviate the sufferings of starving millions) sprung from the genius of science. "The happiness in God's eyes, the last, fleeting vision of those who are condemned. . . . The marrow of our bones is turned to fire, and our veins to threads of flame."[5]

It is this fierce and bleak borderline between hell-fire and heaven's ambiguous radiance, between structures of damnation and the mystery of glory, that Juan Preciado's journey comes to visualise at various levels of space and hollow tenantry, presences-in-absences. The fierce passion and the bleak misery he implies exist more *in cultural outline* than as true holocaust; they exist as outlined cultures of passion and misery at a certain distance from each fossil character in the novel, as if to imply they are as much subjective as objective, felt as non-existent, that their glimmering presence may signify the misconceptions and misreadings within biased cultures of untamable cosmos, until untamable cosmos almost seems to lose authentic equation with undomesticated blessing or fire and to become brute regimes of egocentric flame.

At its most skeletal level Juan Preciado's journey, within the elusive borderline it traces between heaven and hell, is reminiscent of Keatsian 'negative capability' in its visualisation of lives that melt (even as they persist to haunt the womb of space) into the shell of a room or into the sculpture of a wall or into abortive revolutions of sensibility within areas of modern, still ancient, civilisaton.

It was the hour when the children play in the streets in every village, filling the afternoon with their shouts. When the walls still reflect the yellow light of the sun. At least that's what I saw in Sayula yesterday. . . . I also saw the doves *flying in the still air. . . . The shouts of the children flew up like birds.* Now I was here in this *silent* village. [italics mine][6]

Futurity is absent from *Pedro Páramo*. The compression of events is under the domination of time past. Yet the novel is inversely prophetic within the backward-flowing wave of the present that overtakes all characters. It is the vacancies on which Juan Preciado subsists that allow him, as he lies in his grave like one under a Keatsian epitaph bearing names 'writ in water', to converse in articulate fallacy with other grave-dwellers around him who float in the rumourous mind of fiction. The articulation of fallacy touches upon the ultimate pathos of a *structured* immortality. No respite from violence or hate exists in an immortality or freedom replete with incorrigible material bias or material habit. If bias is incorrigible, so is the masquerade of hate through which evil impresarios "betray clowns," in Selden Rodman's phrase. Everything may seem to melt into everything but nothing changes its straitjacketed blind to genuine perception of the spirit of otherness.

That is Pedro Páramo's hell, and it is given surreal shape in the last marriage he contracts—in the wake of a procession of carnival women he has exploited and abused—with Susana, whose voice echoes throughout the novel and is heard early in the fissured body of the narrative as Juan Preciado drifts back into the land of his forefathers and mothers on the wave of museum time or fossil eternity. Or rather, may I say, not so much is she exactly heard as gleaned like a nebulous shine of dew that flashes to speak in the mirror of space. That lightning nebulosity with its vanquished song is substantial with Pedro Páramo's lament. It is as much Juan's voice as Don Pedro's in a rumourous hollow of fiction within closet/mound of earth open to daylight sky as to the constel-lations that fly at night.

I was thinking of you, Susana. . . . When we flew kites. . . . We heard the sounds of the village down below . . . and the wind was tugging the string away from me. "Help me, Susana." And gentle hands grasped my hands. "Let out more string." The wind made us laugh; our glances met while the string played out between our fingers; but it broke, softly, as if it had been struck by the wings of a bird. And up there the paper bird fell in somersaults. . . . Your lips were moist, as if they had been kissing the dew.[7]

We may be reminded, I think, as we reflect on Susana's *Ariel* kite, with its faecal as well as sexual implications, of the gaudy, rainbow costume with which Toomer dresses Muriel and Bernice. We are reminded also of invisible man's scarred mother of freedom and the blues. For Susana is mother of place as well as the unfulfilled *coniunctio* of time, an unfulfilled alchemical marriage in space of bride and bridegroom, which turns into a shroud upon a procession of women and children Don Pedro has abused. And therefore she symbolises a body of sunken futures that regress through her into unfulfilled past lives of other women in whose procession Juan Preciado's mother belongs. Thus it is not surprising, in surreal re-construction, that the arbitrary shadow of Susana falls everywhere like a floating epitaph or floating rumour. Not surprising, in that Susana brings home for the first time in Pedro Páramo's heart (into which Juan Preciado creeps as into a broken closet or mound of stones) the spirit of otherness that begins to haunt him and consume him. For even as he seeks to enfold her, even as she appears to melt into his arms in hell or heaven, he enfolds others he has destroyed, and she too is enfolded by others who stand between him and her essential beauty or tenderness. Hell is the structured hollow embrace that appears to melt into everything, yet to deny him what he seeks with all his life.

Who are the others, in Susana's case, sleeping with her in dream, and deepening the gulf between them? They are as inaccessible and invisible to him—Don Pedro finds—as he is lost to the women he abused whose hell it is to reach endlessly for him and receive nothing but chains on their wrists, contractual obligations that deface their essential freedom to choose, their essential and nebulous exactitude. They are bound by eternity, it seems, to reach for him not out of love but from defaced compassion, and thus their longing reflects the structures that time, false time, has written into immortal, falsely immortal, properties of flesh.

Susana's torments are Don Pedro's only insight into the bonds of terror and hate in which he has entangled himself everywhere. He is an evil impresario who seeks to deceive all with whom he comes into contact by seducing them to invest in illiteracies of the imagination as seals, leases, proud estates/enslavements or passes into eternity. Yet his eminence in the world he rules remains curiously arbitrary. It possesses the arbitrary logic of eternal nightmare. What caprice of time and fate designs him, above all other, in Rulfo's drama, to be supreme tyrant? Are there not others as responsible as he, members of egocentric family, retainers, compliant neighbours, enemies, friends?

One cannot but assume from the ceaseless and self-mocking fate of parodied immortality in Rulfo's fiction that Don Pedro's seduction of others is also central to their obsessions and ambitions, their desire to hug carcasses of time that flow backward into museum space. Thus the arbitrary position he occupies, his eminence as a tyrant, suggests an investment in the hell they share with him, an investment that fixes individual and collective alike, victor and victim alike, into epitaphs of history. They are so fixed they become the ritualised nature of the conquest and the death of mankind within which, nevertheless, a fissure may appear to break the unholy contract between victor and victim, to unravel the gross marriage of cultures or the static masquerade of hell.

Pedro Páramo embodies the masquerade of tyranny to intuit a fissure into collective guilt. Susana is the bride of community that widens that fissure. Juan Preciado is the child-in-father that returns to visit his fatherland/motherland by occupying that fissure.

It is within or against that fissure that ambiguous energy rears its structured caprice into the elements. All structure is comedy or caprice, *Pedro Páramo* appears to imply, useful comedy, diverting caprice, useful institution, fortress or device—provided it is perceived against the incalculable nemesis of space that sees through arbitrary locations of heaven and hell, arbitrary symbols or cultures by which civilisation polarises regimes of victor and victim, rich world and poor world, yet consolidates the insensible marriage of both into an organ of paralysis in the face of world hunger, the waste of war, the horrors of injustice.

Rulfo's parody of heaven and hell would conform to the nihilism of the twentieth century were it not for the intuitive spark of untamable cosmos he plants in Susana, an intamable daybreak, however faint, in the malaise of the entombed senses. "It was the last time I saw you. You passed along the boughs of the paradise trees. . . . Then you disappeared. I cried, 'Come back, Susana!' Pedro Páramo continued to move his lips, to whisper words. Later he closed his mouth and half opened his eyes. They reflected the faint light of daybreak."[8]

The lack of futurity in *Pedro Páramo* may well arouse us to consider the 'death of Man' syndrome that is becoming a fashionable cliché in late twentieth-century intellectualism. The 'death of Man' has been popularised by the French philosopher Michel Foucault. One may gather that one of his prime assertions is that for the Western World "Man is a recent invention" of the late eighteenth century and this "invention" is already obsolete for a variety of reasons.[9] In this context, the retreat from futurity in *Pedro Páramo* is consistent with a parody of history as museum of obsolete man/god.

Yet there is a significant difference between Foucault and Rulfo despite their unconscious alliance. The 'death of Man' in Rulfo's Mexican novel is less gripped by "recent [humanist or deist] invention" and more by compulsions deeply rooted in ancient Mexican myth. Rulfo's fatalism may deepen Foucault's premises into a cross-cultural European and ancient American age.

Ancient America tended to conceal her female muses within traditions whose male gods were so shamanistically fertile, and impregnated with so many supernatural natures, that a tension or contradiction existed in the womb of space, in the principle of motherhood of creation that seemed at times eclipsed by a pre-emptive male strike. In essence, the rainbow bridge or arc of psyche that links partial and obsolescent gods or ages through Quetzalcoatl, Kukulcan, Huracan, Yurokon is a sufficient caveat or warning of the dangers of confusing the death of a particular god with the extinction of metaphysical arts still pregnant with humanity.

Such extinction is ideological fallacy.

The hidden status of the female in pre-Columbian myth—as well as the conscripted and debased faculty of women in modern fiction —does place, as we have seen in Ellison's major novel, in Toomer and in Rulfo, a bleak capacity upon gestating hero or man/god. So it is not surprising to find that ideologies harden into a conviction of the demise of pregnant spirit; once that position is reached the next step, for whatever philosophical reasons, becomes the 'death of Man' in an age of computer-robots and dread of nuclear technology.

The fallacy of the 'death of god and man' may be clear perhaps to the savage mind which wrestles with untamable metaphor and myth, but there is a rationale or ideology, within the post-modern temperament, that is committed to dead myth and tamed metaphor, and this must, unwittingly perhaps, cast a shroud over the womb of space. In part that shroud is the inevitable pollution of the globe by progressive industrialisation. In part it is the obliteration of priceless animal species. In part it is the *mechanics* of birth control. Such mechanics are necessary but they need to come into imaginative equation with revisionary Adamic rib in humanity's side to sacramentalise the price the psyche pays for dislodged fertility.

If Man, as unique spark and complex rib of space, is dead, then the conception of mechanical species becomes in itself an extension of imagination's death. And generations unborn, destined to be locked into envelopes of flesh and certificated names or passes into collective society, are already seized by imagination's epitaph.

Perhaps we are arriving at a juncture where a complex evolution in the arts needs to be visualised; where a conversion of the backward-flowing tide of consciousness needs to be created in depth in order to perceive, in sacramental renascence of species, living futures *through* every sophisticated dead-end or museum fate bound up with adventitious ego.

The paradox of futurity is its intuitive savage/neo-savage play with the notion of a first death and a second death. The first death is a cultural design to fissure the hubris of totality; the second is a psychical design to fissure inner paralysis. And the two 'deaths' (cultural and psychical), in serving to unravel Poesque abortive twinships and to divest the seal of passivity in territorial imperatives and in foetal or mechanical man, are a savage paradox or theme of metaphoric, spiritual re-birth (imagination's re-birth) in theatre of space.

It is as if original poet or painter or composer or sculptor visualises a first death and a second death of the collective imagination in mass-media age, the unravelling of gaudy, funeral materialism followed by the re-dress of inner, polluted, psychical costume, to release profound metaphors and degrees of naked spirit in rich counterpoint.

Can metaphysics of the womb of space recover the creation of Man as spark of untamable cosmos in the wake of diseased, cultural and psychical twinships?

This question deepens and complicates the central vision we are pursuing in this study, namely, the ceaseless mediation of energies between all partial structure masquerading as totality. And thus we resume a deepened exploration of cyclical and vertical dimensions to alter the domination of fiction that flows irreversibly forward or backward. A capacity for glimpses of naked spirit in degrees of rich counterpoint with unravelled shapes or realities may invoke 'doubles' or 'twins'; double (partially interchanged) lives and deaths in the Poesque sense, double (partially interchanged) deprivations to uncover a bridge of forgotten associations between diversity and mutuality, mutual heights/depths, mutual skies/earth, mutual cultures that civilisation has grossly married or eclipsed.

This, I hope, will prove helpful in approaching a particularly complex, long poem *The Double Invention of Komo* by Jay Wright.[10] Komo's nebulous exactitude is manifest early in the poem

By an egg's radiance I arrange my soul's baggage.[11]

That "egg" is intuitively susceptible to various equations with the womb of space. The poem immerses itself in animate versions of the "egg" in womanness attributed to things, "the woman of things."[12]

There are versions that subsist on the elements to imply an open secretion of the senses, buried arousals, inaugurations.[13] Thus rainbow or bridge doubles open and closed memory or secretion, fire and water, into a riddle of dimension in which novel thresholds emerge into, yet beyond, conflicting bonds.

"Another soul's implosion" in the passage of life that doubles into death subsists on a series of rich counterpoint with imageries of danger and hope that sustain glimpsed fractions of spirit residing in "bone" and "umbilical cord" in the woman of things.[14]

As if by cumulative directions and indirections, glimpses of naked spirit move in unravelled gestures of the woman of things. "Spirit's embryo" becomes an enigmatic double of space that reminds one of Ellison's foetal man, though in essence Komo's doubles are the incubation of a dream of genesis rather than the gestation of surrogates of the epic hero within terr torial seal.[15]

The daring brilliance of *The Double Invention of Komo* lies in the poem's immersion in counterpoint, in which activity or alchemy of image gives to structure, as in Rulfo's *Pedro Páramo*, echoes and voices that confess to caprice. But Wright's focus lives with—and makes poetry from a failure to seize—the unseizable future, and in so doing half-cycles, half-unravels, immediate intuition into a "trembling that bells" or summons what is to come, absent yet present double, unseizable god's double of visible light and invisible psyche that is 'open' frame, 'open' seal, upon a riddle of descending frames and biases into an animate cosmos, a capricious anvil.[16]

The rhythms of *Komo* appear to veer at times on many planes and grooves of sensation; this is its extraordinary quality as well as difficulty in range and act. That difficulty, however, is rich with potential once one perceives that there lurks within and beneath the poem an arbitration of risk that mediates between form and spirit to play with animist model or structure as necessary traps of sensibility, so plumbed they oscillate capacities for fissure and relief.

In Wright's afterword to his long epic poem he acknowledges his indebtedness, in the arrangement of the poem under various principles of initiation, to "a group of French anthropologists, associated with Marcel Griaule, on an expedition to Dakar and Djibouti beginning in 1929 and subsequent expeditions to Mali, Chad, and Cameroon." His deliberate usage of Komo initiation/creation myth is of great interest. Emphasis in this study is on the active and original imagery of the poem, as this associates itself readily with the stage in our explorations of cultural/psychical counterpoint into rich degrees of naked spirit.

The Sky of Fiction

Wide Sargasso Sea by Jean Rhys varies the rainbow arc between cultures in a profoundly intuitive spirit.[17] To appreciate that variation we need to recall the bridge between sky of fiction and earth's womb of space that is implicit in the rainbow arc from Central to South America in Quetzalcoatl (snake and bird) and Yurokon (Quetzalcoatl's Carib cousin). Then we need to compress that bridge into a different set of features.

The foodbearing tree of the world in Arawak and Macusi legend reaches to the sky of fiction across forgotten ages, but we become suddenly aware of it as creation bridge or myth between sky and earth at a time of catastrophe when a new genesis or vision has become necessary.

It is a time of war. The rainbow compression of a tree is set on fire by the Caribs when the Arawaks seek refuge in its branches, upon which stand multi-coloured birds and fruit overcast in the wake of the fire by a cloud of smoke. Creation suffers and needs to be re-dressed if the spirit of the stars is to be discovered again. The fire rages and ascends even higher to drive the Arawaks up and up until there is no further escape, they burn and rise into a spark in the sky of fiction. That spark becomes the seed of the garden of the Pleiades.

The foodbearing tree, therefore, is re-dressed, the blackened fruit unravelled into a garden in the sky of fiction. The most curious enigma of all is the reconciliation that the Caribs and Arawaks appear to achieve, a treaty of sensibility that borders on *coniunctio* between sky and earth.

These motifs of the womb of space are converted by inner necessity—intuitive necessity—into original variables in *Wide Sargasso Sea*. First, let us note the fire-motif in the creation myth; second, the psyche of war and catastrophe in which the foodbearing tree is rooted; third, the sparked garden of *coniunctio* in the sky of fiction.

There is a persistent fire-motif that runs through the fabric of *Wide Sargasso Sea* in counterpoint to legacies of slavery and conquest in the soil of the Caribbean. Antoinette and her relations are landowners yet they are pursued characters, pursued by ex-slaves who set fire to their property, pursued by rumours of nervous inheritance and madness. Rumour is a cycle, a ripple, as in Rulfo's *Pedro Páramo, set in motion by doubles of fiction. Antoinette is the double of mad Bertha, the white-West Indian* creole who married the Englishman Rochester in Charlotte Brontë's *Jane Eyre*.

Mad Bertha's madness is so absolute in *Jane Eyre* that her life is a living death. Jean Rhys re-dresses mad Bertha, re-names her Antoinette. The re-dress is extreme. It comes to an incredible climax at the heart of fire when Antoinette appears to rise above her enemies and to see "the sky . . . the tree of life in flames. . . . It was red and all my life was in it."[18] It would seem to me that in re-dressing the Charlotte Brontë fictional constellation of Rochester and Bertha, Jean Rhys is involved in a subtle, however intuitive *coniunctio*, an immaterial reconciliation, between divided bride and bridegroom whose honeymoon in be-devilled plantation or foodbearing tree becomes an ultimatum of distress.

The intuitive correspondence *Wide Sargasso Sea* achieves with Arawak/Macusi creation myth and foodbearing tree is remarkable and there are other subtle variables that further highlight Jean Rhys's originality in depth. I shall come to these in a moment, but first a word or two about references to the creation myth I have outlined.

There is a reference to it in Walter Roth's essays on Guianese folklore, and in Claude Lévi-Strauss's *The Raw and the Cooked*. The substance of the tale tends to vary a little with each interpreter. Roth's climate of interpretation is closer to Frazer's biases in the *Golden Bough*, Lévi-Strauss is concerned with complex equations between nature (the raw) and culture (the cooked). I have been stressing doubles in untamable cosmos to bridge a divide.

One of the most remarkable variables of re-dressed psyche in *Wide Sargasso Sea* resides in the subtle play or emphasis upon ambiguous 'death' (psychical design to fissure the hubris of totality) in regard to Bertha and her double Antoinette, and also to Bertha's husband Rochester.

First of all, mad Bertha of *Jane Eyre* is confined in Thornfield Hall where Rochester casts a shroud over her. He relegates her to the 'dead' and perceives himself as a 'widower' tied to stone. That state of psychical widowhood is threaded by Jean Rhys into her novel with a difference however, for she deepens Antoinette's aloneness to convert Rochester's action into stone-hearted caprice. This is a reversal of Charlotte Brontë's characterisation.

We begin to move into a new capacity. For that reversal goes deeper than a mere turning of the tables. Rochester's hubris is a form of death in himself but it has conscripted Bertha and has sown

paralysis. Bertha's double, Antoinette in *Wide Sargasso Sea*, turns
to her black Haitian nurse Christophine for help from the earth-
gods who tend the foodbearing tree that grows to heaven, and
asks for a love potion to bring him back to life in her bed.

I think one is justified in seeing in Christophine's *obeah* or
Voodoo potion a link with Arawak foodbearing tree, though such
a link is not explicit in *Wide Sargasso Sea*. Nevertheless the alchemy of image and word throughout the text of the narrative, the
varied emphases on "tree" and "the garden of my Spouse," the
catholicity of elements in the soil of the Caribbean—all lend themselves to a deepened apprehension of Haitian *obeah* (as masked
branch or antidote to the death of love).

Christophine, the Haitian nurse, is banished by "Rochester" from
his West Indian household as an evil witch or *obeah* woman. More
important, Christophine herself knows that the potion she
concocted was of dubious virtue, that love is not to be coerced into
resurrection, and that it is not in her gift to restore "Rochester"
(who is never named in *Wide Sargasso Sea*) to Antoinette's arms.
Such drugged restoration is a psychical fallacy. Antoinette mourns,
"I hear him every night walking up and down the verandah. Up
and down. When he passes my door he says, Goodnight, Bertha.
He never calls me Antoinette now. . . . And I dream. *Then I beat
my fist on a stone.* Going away to Martinique or England or
anywhere else, that is the lie . . ." [italics mine].[19]

Jean Rhys's parents were a Welsh father and a white West Indian
creole mother. Her imaginative inheritances were 'white' and 'black'
in tone within a Caribbean catholicity that includes Haitian *vodun*
or Voodoo and many versions or energetic translations of
Christianity. *Obeah* remains a pejorative term in that it reflects a
state of mind or embarrassment over addictions to magic,
necessary hell-fire or purgatory through which to re-enter 'lost'
origins, 'lost' divinity.

It is Christophine, in particular, who symbolises the forbidden
obeah strain in Jean Rhys's imagination that would goad
"Rochester" back to life after he has 'widowed' and abandoned
Bertha/Antoinette, while like a dead man still formally alive, he
paces the verandah.

In strict Roman Catholic context (in contradistinction to alchemy
and catholicity of origins) we need to glance at the Roman Catholic
convent in which Antoinette spent an impressionable period after

her home was set on fire by angry ex-slaves, a fire that precipitated a nervous breakdown in her mother Annette (also known as Bertha) and occasioned the death of Pierre, the youngest member of the family. It is here, in the convent, that we begin to perceive the depth of subversion or ecstatic hunger that begins to envelop Antoinette, to prepare her, so to speak, to become the bride of a spiritual *obeah* bull or inferior double of god. During the doomed honeymoon between "Rochester" and Antoinette, before he abandons her and widows her on the marriage-bed, he is given "a cup of bull's blood" by Antoinette. The symbolic potion is of no avail. It confirms his coming retreat into the "stone" or "relic" of ecstasy. Yet it is of importance in that it recalls to Antoinette her earlier life in the convent when she contemplates Roman Catholic relics, and the elusive life of precarious divinity in such relics, as if in anticipation of the relic of ecstasy "Rochester" becomes after his symbolic draught, a relic that may yield its stone-function to immaterial re-animation in the sky of fiction above the "tree of life in flames," where relics are consumed and redeemed.[20]

The "tree of life" makes one of its appearances in the convent and bears "a rose from the garden of my Spouse." It is a rose saturated with indebtedness to the black soil of dreams in which Antoinette seeks to "hold up [her] dress, it trails in the dirt, my beautiful dress." The dream continues, "We are no longer in the forest but in an enclosed garden. . . . I stumble over my dress and cannot get up. I touch a tree and my arms hold on to it. 'Here, here.' But I think I will not go any further. The tree sways and jerks as if it is trying to throw me off. Still I cling and the seconds pass and each one is a thousand years. 'Here, in here,' a strange voice said, and the tree stopped swaying and jerking."[21]

Antoinette's indebtedness to the "rose of my Spouse" and to soil of dreams is a preparation for a dialogue with the 'other' in the garden, the strange dark terrifying voice within and without her that she never forgets. It is a voice that celebrates and mourns her coming betrothal and marriage. For it is less the stranger she marries and more intimately herself who tastes "the cup of bull's blood" Christophine offers her uncomprehending bridegroom. It is a voice that pushes her beyond the walls of convent or school in which she shelters. In the darkness of that voice, the nuns in the school have "cheerful faces" she resents. They do not understand her magical "spouse." They do not perceive a richer catholicity beneath the formal Catholic education they dispense. Their religion, however evocative in its relics, has become a respectable ritual, an undemanding ornament, as undemanding or frozen in posture as the Greek or Roman goddess of the Milky Way from whose breasts the white fluid spurts across the sky into the calloused mouth of a consumer age.

Whereas the "bull's blood" of art and religion is an imagistic confession of a cross-cultural labyrinth, the transformation of apparently incorrigible bias in all mankind tests and challenges the imagination beyond ideal formula. It is the stigma of complex earthiness and exile from convention. It is raised with anguish into the stars. Bertha doubles into Antoinette to secure a hidden surrender of being, a loss of soul to find soul, an overturning of ritual-for-the-sake-of-ritual to enhance sensibility and feeling, a disrupted voice of convention in order to find (or begin to find) the voice in the foodbearing tree.

These considerations are never explicitly stated in *Wide Sargasso Sea*. Their authenticity lies, I find, in a measure of confused force that drives her to say to one of the nuns before she leaves the convent, "I dreamed I was in Hell." The nun replies, "That dream is evil. Put it from your mind—never think of it again."[22] But she was to dream and think of it again and again. And the nun's incomprehension is woven into Bertha's shroud and apparent damnation. It was Antoinette's passion to illumine by fire the other's essential humanity and precarious *coniunctio* with layers of the past that had tormented her.

FIVE
The Whirling Stone

Extremity and Likeness

The narrow basis of realism, as an art that mirrors common-sense day or pigmented identity, tends inevitably to polarise cultures or to reinforce eclipses of otherness within legacies of conquest that rule the world. In so doing it also voids a capacity for the true marriage of like to like within a multi-cultural universe. The latter conviction may seem unjustified, at first sight, until one reflects deeply upon it.

Like does mirror like in realistic portraiture, but this is not the case with *The Double Invention of Komo* and *Wide Sargasso Sea*. Neither mirrors the other in like rhetoric or appearance, yet a significant, moving likeness exists when one perceives the extremities that live in each work, extremities of active and subtle modification of dense texture in *Komo* (thus a 'point' or subtle double lives within the cloak Komo wears), extremities of immaterial animation within accumulative design concealing character from character in *Wide Sargasso Sea* (thus a 'point' or immaterial focus lives in the anthropomorphic stone relics of *Wide Sargasso Sea*). The pitch of extremity in both poem and novel lays bare therefore a complex point through which unsuspected parallels move in the nightsky of tradition.

Rochester and mad Bertha are static accumulative attire and also a subtle, interior, parallel animation in Jean Rhys's re-dress of Charlotte Brontë's polarisations; a tree of fire arises that invokes subtle parallel 'trees' and 'fires' into the re-dress of static, fictional constellation. *Komo* also is susceptible to a visionary point through which a parallel spark from an anvil of initiations runs into the eye of space and into a body of futurity.

Thus a cross-cultural web and likeness are revealed in novel and poem through points that unravel apparently incompatible appearances between Komo and Antoinette to create unsuspected parallels. Komo and Antoinette run in the sky of fiction as sparked lines within anvil or stone. The catholicity of *Wide Sargasso Sea* turns into subtle *coniunctio* of cultures that address the sparked cradle of Komo.

All this is unfathomably rooted in the paradoxes and unconscious ironies of asymmetric infinity or creation myth.

The politics of culture assume that like to like signifies a monolithic cradle or monolithic origin. Whereas in creative subtlety or re-dress and interior animation, involving both density and immaterial or mental point, monoliths are extremes/extremities that become fissures of emotion in claustrophobic and historical or cultural space, when imbued with asymmetric spirit or intangible, untamable life. Those fissures are parallels, extensions, as I have said before, in and into bodies of experience whose mental point or core of likeness turns into the spark or passion of science and art.

In this context of nebulous spark or exactitude of passion, the "rose in the garden of my Spouse" of which Antoinette dreams matches the garden of the Pleiades in Arawak mythology. One is the other's flare of extremity, and in so being runs backward and forward into the mystery of original light and darkness, in which 'Catholic rose' and 'savage star' are *partial* signatures or fictions of the birth of undying creation and truth.

In previous chapters I stressed unstructured mediation, whereas now one varies medium or metaphor into a point where exactitude doubles or may treble or quadruple, perhaps *ad infinitum*, to provide ceaseless parallel animations or subtle likenesses *through* contrasting densities or opposite and varied appearances. Both (unstructured mediation and mental point) are alike but they vary the sensation of naked spirit arbitrating mythically, ungraspably, between accumulations of order or habit or calloused fates in which the 'death of Man' occurs.

Paule Marshall's *The Chosen Place, the Timeless People* appeared about three years after *Wide Sargasso Sea* was published and there, in the very gateway of the novel we meet a skeleton-masked character, a 'death of Man' symbol. Merle Kinbona, queen of the folk of Bourne Island, stops her car at a bad section of poor road over which she has been driving with a woman companion, Leesy, and confronts Mr Douglin, "his black skin sucked in upon the skeletal frame of his face and his eyes like two cleanly bored holes that had been blasted out of the skull with a gun."[1]

Bourne Island (an imaginary island in the Caribbean Sea) compounds traits and tendencies in the diseased body-politic of West Indian societies. Douglin is as much a roadmender as a doorkeeper into the kingdom of the living dead, which in its extremity resembles invisible man's asylum of the Golden Day in Bledsoe's incestuous Trueblood territory.

The galvanic momentum that tends to seize the novel, and which is apparent at the very outset in Merle Kinbona's battered car, the regal corpse of a car that she drives, that she brakes and stops by the skin of its teeth from "hurtling onto the empty roadbed where it would have been hopelessly mired for days perhaps, in a thick bog of mud and broken marl," masks a far deeper compulsion into elemental and subconscious furies and rebellions within the funereal gaiety and carnival world of Bournehills.[2]

The curious extremity of ambivalent rebellion in *The Chosen Place, the Timeless People*, touches a 'point' that allows us to chart a parallel to Poe's *Pym* and the succession of abortive mutinies against captain(s) block. In Paule Marshall's novel, the ground of failed mutiny is less obvious, the hierarchy of block commanders of the globe less sensational or immediately apparent. The emphasis upon commander and commanded actually shifts into a disequilibrium between commanding, material culture (associated with the rich, Western world) and commanded, subject crew (associated with ex-slave, colonial world). That shift adorns itself in the mechanics of the age, machinery, technology, into which is fed a Bournehills Icarus falling in the sky of civilisation. The 'flying motif' is well established in the oral traditions of African/American slave longing for wings with which to return 'home'. It plays a part in Anancy or flying trickster folklore. Thus Icarus Anancy runs parallel to Odysseus Anancy (see Chapter Three) as cross-cultural body arching through mutated African cultures into mutated ancient Greek myth.

It seems to me essential to trace the gradient, so to speak, of the Icarus Anancy fall, as herein lies the subtle clue that bears with paradoxical substantiality upon Paule Marshall's intuitive imagination.

At the outset of our inquiry into gradient or curvature of the fall, one needs to declare that, despite assertions made throughout *The Chosen Place, the Timeless People* reflecting a conservative posture or resistance to change in the Bournehills population, the shape of the narrative is far less strictly dependent on a linkage to nineteenth-century doubles than is the case in *Wide Sargasso Sea*. It is less strictly linked to antecedent doubles, in that the accumulation of historical detail is more *ad hoc* in essence and tone, a more fictional, documentary report on a beleaguered, island people than a neo-classical, comedy-of-manners convention. Yet, for this very reason, a paradox emerges to illumine the two novels in cross-cultural context. The documentary substance of *The Chosen Place, the Timeless People* is capable of dislodging itself into moments of intense anguish, and an *avant-garde* persuasion, in the militant sense, strikes sparks in characters to make links into the past where one would not judge them to be, save in extremity and cross-cultural context.

Paule Marshall's parents were mixed West Indian creoles but she was born in Brooklyn, New York, and her novel is more political in tone than Jean Rhys's characterisations with their class-or-wealth fixated background. In extremity, however, the wealth-fixation built into Jean Rhys's Antoinette matches an obsessional spark—an esoteric folk security—in Paule Marshall's Merle Kinbona.

In extremity again, a complex point is created in which Antoinette and Merle run parallel to each other, and Merle conceals a 'Bertha-madness' in herself. She tends to suffer traumas of distress that she exorcises by irrational conjunctions of sensitivity and creative ruthlessness that are a kind of therapeutic *obeah*. The pressure is acute. For instance, it rises when she discovers that the delay on the road—her meeting with the death-masked roadmender—has robbed her of time to drive to the airport and meet Allen Fuso; she rings a friend, distinguished lawyer Lyle Hutson, to persuade him to go in her place. Hutson is conscripted by her charisma when she projects into him, over the telephone, a vision of child-starvation and "duppy," ex-slave or ghost regimes built into the academic lights of Bournehills, the "legal luminaries" who appear to have forgotten their antecedents. It is a nimble ultimatum, a half-playful, half-threatening curse upon the establishment; thus, she persuades the Lyle Hutsons and others and at the same time balances her sanity on a precipice of emotion. " 'Lyle, are you there. . . . Don't try to play Mr Big with me because you know what I think about all you legal luminaries with . your duppy nightgowns and musty wigs. . . . I've had to pay with my sanity for the right to speak my mind so you know I must talk. . . .' "[3] Still talking, she acquires in her voice a down-hill tone that seems to race with the shadow of itself, "she begins backing towards a window close by, drawn there by a sound that could have been the low, unremitting whirr of the heat slowly rising, now that it is past noon, to a new and ominous high. 'Oh, crime, the plane!' "[4]

We intimated in the last chapter that 'immaterial animation' or 'mental point' within *Wide Sargasso Sea* lay within the conservative facade through which it gleamed, but such gleam or spark in *The Chosen Place, the Timeless People* is a relic of the fall of Anancy Icarus. On the broad face of the novel, the Bournehills folk resistance to change resembles social fate or comedy-of-manners cement, but it is much more consistent with a subconscious confession of fears of block commanders of the globe—commanding, brute technology that mirrors the sea and the land to provide, as in a dream, the summit of fascination by which Icarus is driven, the deceptions and furies (man-made fire, dream-made darkness in apparent twinship with a sun of technology) through which he plunges to his death.

Thus the substantial resistance to change in the Bournehills "timeless people" becomes a tension, a pointed anguish, on the curvature of fall; it dresses itself in feared and reactionary technology that is perpetually on the verge of collapse and bordering upon a blind and nihilist resistance to innovative science and art. As such it involuntarily exposes adventitious "timeless order" built on terror of the unknown.

It also exposes the largely abortive inner and outer rebellion it stages against repressive history, which continues to feed on perennial anxiety as much as on economic deprivation. I say 'largely abortive' because a slender tissue of evolving potential emerges, the total collapse of *ad hoc* colonial cement is offset by a spark of evolutionary sensibility in Merle Kinbona's ecstatic madness, when the novel closes, though she herself, as muse of re-birth and change, remains hedged by intractable circumstance, and her mind and heart remain in pawn to the curvature of the fall of Anancy Icarus.

In the curvature of that fall lies a failed marriage of commanding heights with anxiety-ridden depths, a failed mutiny as well against the sun of technology. Merle Kinbona's involvement with the Bournehills folk is a paradox. She is a pregnant muse of the people, she sustains *avant-garde* (or militant, forward) hope to achieve the re-birth of the depths in the heights, but at the same time her enlargement of ambition is akin to a gross envelope of deprivation and misgiving masquerading as a pregnant or swollen feature.

Before resuming the thread of latent paradox within *The Chosen Place, the Timeless People*, it may be helpful to review some of the considerations expressed before in regard to the dual death of Man, a *cultural* death followed by a *psychical* death as threshold to the savage paradox of spiritual re-birth (with its implications of re-dressed psyche or art of renascence).

Savage paradox of spirit subsists on the conversion of deprivations. The 'enlarged body of fears' in the Bournehills folk is a deprivation, a conscription, that carries nevertheless a latent conversion within folk queen Merle into militant pregnancy or annunciation of courage in child of the gestating future.

In previous chapters we saw how parable depends on the conversion of deprivations into complex freedom and truth. What is at stake, it seems to me, is a vision of metamorphosis. An enlarged folk-body that feeds, alas, on terror may metamorphose into pregnant, individual courageous art that seeks no facile or corrupt popular support. That metamorphosis or conversion is the alchemisation of terror into a profound encounter with reality. It carries the thrust not only of *avant-garde* premonition but of genuine originality and insight, re-dressed relations between partial images, whether these be fear-images or pregnancy-of-humanity images. It is a ravelling/unravelling art, ravelled/unravelled cloak, with ravelled/unravelled enlargements and new angles of vision in a ceaseless (however apparently unfulfilled) marriage between heights and depths in order to plumb a *potency of spirit*.

Potency of spirit: this is the crucial mediation between the apparently uniform past and the apparently obscure future that converts the dual death of Man. The first cultural death of Man has individual and social faces. An example of the individual (half-stylised and subtly collective) face appears in the doomed marriage of Bertha and Rochester. An example of the social (subtly technologic) face appears in the doomed machinery of the doomed canefield/plantation industry of the Bournehills people.

The first cultural death is inevitably followed by inner atrophy or psychical funeral. Built-in expectations (stylised in individual habit and other collective formula) begin to fall in the wake of the first economic domino. Note that in placing such extreme, apparently doom-laden stresses upon 'faces', whether individual, social or economic, one needs to re-emphasise that one is involved in the paradox of resources of variables of the imagination through which the past speaks to the present and to the future. One's complex faith lies, in this context, in the deep-seated life of a work of the imagination, its inner capacity for re-dressed bodies and imageries, a re-dress significantly illumined by cross-cultural perspective. Bertha and Rochester possess in themselves, within the genius of Charlotte Brontë, the seed of such re-dress, but the seminal force of the fiction as a whole, structured as it is by comedy-of-manners cultural homogeneity, tends to be overshot by a morality sensible to property and money but insensible to the acute 'madness', so to speak, of human longing and hope in a ravaged and bewildered world from which one has profited but to which one remains blind. The seminal force of arbitrating genius is never entirely vanquished and it comes into play within a re-dressed dialogue with reality in Jean Rhys's Antoinette's sargasso sea sky-fiction that is it-self fertilised by the intuitive equation it carries with Caribbean/Arawak foodbearing tree. The shadow of re-dress is equally at stake in invisible man's descent into nightmare foetus and into intuitive, cannibal cross-culture from Yurokon to the Cyclops. This bears in its extremity on enlarged folk-body in *The Chosen Place, the Timeless People*.

Mental Fire and Bride of Earth

The plane on which Allen Fuso arrives, about which Merle Kinbona telephones a "legal luminary," also brings Anancy Icarus Vere, great-nephew of Leesy with whom Kinbona had been driving when she brakes her car suddenly and confronts the roadmender and doorkeeper to the kingdom of the living dead.

There are two other passengers on the plane, Saul and Harriet Amron. Saul Amron is a Jewish social scientist with whom American-Polish Allen Fuso works. As Saul reposes on the plane he reveals "all his physical flaws to anyone who cared to look." In Allen Fuso is laid bare "a suggestion of tremendous *unused* power in the arms and legs, shoulders and back" [italics mine].[5]

All are, in one degree or another, subjects of the nightsky of a civilisation in which a mental sun burns to melt their wings. In their unused or collapsed extremity, they stand in need of a genuine *coniunctio* of mental fire and shadow of earth that flies with the rain and the river and the sea. Their spiritual need to fly, to evolve wings in the wake of some unstated, cultural/psychical castration, is not at all obvious but it runs in Vere's blood to illumine the shadow of half-atrophy, half-genius, in theirs.

We are introduced to Vere, as the small two-engined plane they had boarded at Puerto Rico after a flight from the United States, begins to descend. Vere feels acutely "the sudden drop and shudder in the pit of his stomach." It is a sensation that seems calculated to sharpen an earlier echo, Merle Kinbona's braked descent in her royal corpse of a car on Mr Douglin's road. The parallel between Kin-bona's car (reminiscent of Komo's convertible bone into umbilical cord) and Vere's dream-chariot tightens as the plane descends; Vere is possessed by an ominous inkling or memory of falling "into a deep pit." The mixed tenses of past event, clairvoyant future, and present foreboding, are triggered in part by the recall of "great-aunt Leesy's husband crushed to death in the deep pit which housed the rollers [that were] used to extract the juice from the cane" and in part by a dream he cherishes of driving his own car in the Whitmonday Motor Race on the island.[6] It is a dream in which he already sees himself stripping down a car and refleshing its bones close to heart's blood, close to mental fire of wings that he nurses within the shadow/cave of his body.

Let us look at the parallels that run through 'points' of extremity that are now visible in the 'womb of space': First, the extremity of 'queen' Merle's encounter with the doorkeeper of the 'living dead' in her regal corpse of a car; second, great-aunt Leesy's husband's descent into the cane-pit; third, Vere's dream-car close to heart's blood, heart's land and sea. Taken together they constitute the latitude and amplitude of fears, memories and premonitions built into the folk, save that they point obscurely, problematically, through heart's juice, land, sea, air, fire, to the conversion of massive deprivation into evolutionary spectre, figurative womb of the elements, pregnant space.

That tension between the elements, as carnival or spectral figure, and the implicit collapse of an age, as embodied fact, is the half-symbolic, half-factual curve of the novel that touches all the characters to imbue them with mental ambiguity. It is a distinction that a reader may easily miss because the apparent realism of the novel would tend to identify the author's intentions with *traumatic resistances to change* that become statically embodied and dominant in the way one tended to perceive a seal or dominance of Cyclopean nightmare in Ellison's Bledsoe regimes, or an arbitrary fixture of museum scapegoat in Rulfo's *Pedro Páramo*. But as soon as one perceives the *ad hoc* nature of ex-slave, ex-colonial cement in *The Chosen Place, the Timeless People* in cross-culture with sparks of anguish, one realises that a necessity for innovative form is at stake, however unconscious it is to itself in partial straitjacket or block of resistance.

Merle is the catalyst of potential heights in depths within the seal or envelope of folk dread: she links sparks or evolutionary points within the bloodstream of space.

That linkage begins with great-aunt Leesy and Vere. Merle is immersed in pathology of these characters. On one hand, there is the old woman's folk-resistance to (implicit mutiny against) her nephew's designs to build a car; on the other, there are Vere's emotions and ambitions that are compounded of obsession with the car and also with a blighted love affair that festers in his imagination as if it seeks to be ground into folk-soil, folk-roadways, over which he hopes to race his engine. Merle as folk-queen, as *obeah*-queen, suffers in concrete abstract, so to speak, the fate that Vere would mete out to soil or kingdom.

The intuitive ground of blighted love in earth-bride and *obeah*-

queen beneath the friction of wheels or wings sustains an obscure thrust as well into the cane-pit in which great-aunt Leesy's husband fell. It is another pointer into extreme arc or tension between death and life, between the widowhood that Leesy endures and the trauma of blighted love beneath flying wheels that Merle plays in unconscious folk theatre. No wonder she suffers fiery illnesses and losses of memory.

Leesy is shackled by the death of her husband. It has left her inwardly scarred and suspicious of technology; pit of the sun that bled him physically, now bleeds her mentally. Indeed Leesy's pattern of double existences, past physical death of her lost husband (which she incorporates into herself), impending death of her doomed great-nephew (that she secretes as psychical event in her imagination), makes her a curious pawn of spirit in the kingdom of the living dead, at whose gate we meet her in Merle's company when the novel begins.

Vere is shackled by the woman he had loved and the inverted' child she had borne him. He is tied to the obstinate, "duppy" (child-ghost) kingdom of the living dead from which he had travelled to the United States to escape for a while to make his fortune, but to which he had returned to blighted paternity, blighted fortune of love, in the woman who had turned her back upon him. Their unfruitful *coniunctio* is nevertheless the seed of re-visioned fossil-child, re-visioned foetus, re-visioned, live, fossil birth of wings with which to fly once again from the kingdom of the dead into the sun.

Such a view of the novel may be gleaned from relics of the universal arc that one associates with Anancy Icarus Vere and with queen Merle, in whom exists the macrocosmic rather than microcosmic identity of protuberant yet inconclusive pawn that each character is to the other.

On completion of the racing car of his dreams that he paints a fiery red to rival the blood of the sun, Vere drives into the district where the mother of his dead child lives. It is Carnival time on the island. He finds her in her room painting herself for the dance. The room is filled with dolls. She herself, as unconscious subject of Merle's *obeah* regime, is like a doll, *a large, bird-like doll*. Vere raises a cane and strikes her. "The blow [that he delivers] catches her *and she folds in like a bird*" [italics mine].[7] Thus we may pluck from the narrative, by visualising certain extremities of emotion, both 'wings' and 'foetus'. We need to give these 'points' particular emphasis within the enlarged and voluminous chapter from which they arise. They are, I believe, genuine relics of the curvature of emotion that ties Icarus Anancy to thread of capacity and to winged spectre in the bride and queen of fate.

One must confess that Paule Marshall does not pursue this clue when she comes later in her novel to the death of Vere. She sees Vere's overturned car as a wilful horse that betrays and kills its master. In broad outline this faults the Icarus bird-motif that I have put forward, but in extremity it endorses an animal passion, a savage half-regressive, half-revolutionary spectre, whether bird or horse, within the blood of the sun, within fossil, live doll, and within anthropomorphic car and polluted fire that kicks like a strangled yet untamable beast.

Thus the curve of Anancy Icarus gleams with involuntary 'points' of irony, re-visioned foetus of lost child (winged doll), re-visioned animal fire in the soil of the kingdom of the dead. It creates a tension of convertible deprivations, death overshadowed by mysterious ground of spirit within relics of the past. In this context, I find *The Chosen Place, the Timeless People* to be a work that confirms what is implicit in the thrust of an inquiry through cross-cultural extremity in several strangely parallel fictions; namely, the accent upon 'negative capability' in dead-end realism, a realism made narrow by egocentric histories that need to be creatively disrupted by pressures of infinity within the womb of space if that realism is to yield insight into 'inverted' metamorphoses as threshold to a higher aesthetic factor in pawns of spirit.

On the day of the race, "his smile widening," Vere flew ahead of his rivals. A "surprised roar went up as he took the lead . . . the same stunning hosannah of his imagining, a sound like the roaring of his own blood in his ears." The race was "his (the crowd was already proclaiming him the undisputed winner) when he felt the first tremor. It was like a horse grown restive under too tight a rein. . . ."[8]

The arc of Vere's flight and fall exists in staggered phases throughout the novel. As one considers relics associated with it one may, I think, establish parallels through apparently like or unlike

character. The Americans Saul and Harriet Amron, and Allen
Fuso, are entangled in a dimension of folk-character, folk-
deprivation, however sophisticated they seem as individual
outsiders in Bourne Island. They are entangled in the *obeah* of the
folk subconsciously or unconsciously.

Harriet, Saul's over-ambitious wife, is swept like a sudden,
inflated doll, a perverse fertility symbol, into the "timeless" sea.
She runs parallel to Vere's "riverbed" into which the Icarus bird-
horse fell. An emotional flood erupts amidst a Carnival torrent of
people that sweeps her along on its crest. Saul is caught in the web
of intrigue that she engineers; his blindness or inner paralysis
collapses into Merle's arms, which seem to hold Vere's phantom
shattered body as well. When Merle leaves the island at the end of
the novel, her drive to the airport past Mr Douglin—the "keeper of
the grave"—is little more than ritual gesture to dead-end rebels of
slave history whose mutiny has collapsed. Even so, in their
extremity, another intuitive reading is available to us, those dead-
end rebels may be seen as illumined sparks or relics of Vere's
"timeless" fall, Merle's lost mental sons and mental husbands of
fire.[9]

Merle's state of mental 'widowhood' resembles, yet differs from,
Antoinette's in *Wide Sargasso Sea*. Whereas Antoinette is fired into
immaterial re-marriage to a stone bridegroom *ascending* into the
sparked sky of creation myth, Merle is less ascending 'widow' into
re-dressed bride and more 'psychically pregnant form' upon an arc
of Icarus Anancy fire *descending* from the sky of slave rebels into
extremities of paradox.

It is fascinating at this stage to look at further implications that
reside in mental widow, psychical bride and child by turning to
another deceptively realist novel, *Voss*, by the great Australian
novelist Patrick White.

Paradoxes of Form

We need, I think, to approach the issue of 'pregnant form' in
Voss through Laura Trevelyan, a middle-class Australian woman
of the mid-nineteenth century. *Voss* was published in the mid-
twentieth century but its setting is mid-nineteenth-century
Australia. Voss is a fictional incarnation of Ludwig Leichardt who

died in the Australian desert in 1848. Thus a "doubling star," historic and fictional, threads its way into the twentieth-century Australian sky of legend.

Laura Trevelyan is linked in the novel to Voss, on one hand, and to Rose Portion, on the other. Rose Portion is Laura's emancipist servant who becomes pregnant by a harlequin *journeyman* figure, Jack Slipper, who is an inverse pawn to Voss, the proud and complex *explorer*. Laura, therefore, in extremity sustains many curious parallels through apparently like and unlike character. In her emancipist servant Rose, whose child is to become Voss's psychical child, and her adopted daughter, she strikes roots not only into Australia's convict era but also into anecdotal, rather than strictly historical, layers that flit through the Australian imagination in the shape of elusive, harlequin Jack Slipper.

Slipper is an earthy, inferior shadow, as it were, of the burnished skeleton of Voss in the sky of Australian legend. Before Voss leaves for the Outback, where he is to be consumed by earth and sky, Laura embraces him as if he were already dead and the earth reels beneath them to take his bones into the stars. "In the passion of their relationship, she had encountered his wrist. She held his bones. All their gestures had ugliness, convulsiveness in common. They stood with their legs apart inside their innocent clothes, the better to grip the reeling earth."[10] The shadow or double that Voss casts, in that embrace, flits into the body of Jack Slipper whose intercourse with Rose plants the seed Laura accepts as *psychically fertile* within Voss and herself. It is an embrace that also lays bare the hubris of Faustian will that cuts him off, in himself, from earthy shadow or flesh-and-blood contact. She says:

"I shall think of you with alarm. . . . To maintain such standards of pride, in the face of what you must experience on this journey, is truly alarming."

"I am not in the habit of setting myself limits."

"Then I will learn to pray for you."[11]

Laura also reflects, in her friends, family and relations, the passivity of a growing, moneyed class in Australia, its divorce from the long shadow of Asia despite its investment in the 'womb of the future' within "mental travellers" (in Blake's phrase) upon whom hang potential generations within ambivalences of fear and hope.

"Mental traveller" encompasses Laura herself since she becomes a hallucinated figure, in Voss's expedition, with whom he secretly converses as he travels deeper and deeper into the Outback. She is constantly at his side however invisible she may be to his companions. By the same token, Laura 'lives' Voss's life and death within the womb of space. She is wed to him in a bloodstream of events as in a dream of a foetus gestating in her own body, parallelling Rose Portion's pregnancy and death in giving birth to the child she conceived with Voss's shadow or double.

The novelistic structure of *Voss* has certain resemblances to comedy-of-manners fiction that one associates with *Wide Sargasso Sea* or with *Jane Eyre*. It possesses also some degree of folk resistance to change that we perceived in *The Chosen Place, the Timeless People*. But, in extremity, it yields a parallel one would not expect to find to Rulfo's *Pedro Páramo*. That parallel is rooted in paradox and it acquaints us with the far-reaching kinships inherent in the concept of *mental traveller*.

The hollow village territory populated by ghosts, to which Rulfo's mental traveller Juan Preciado returns from a future that has been overturned by *avant-garde* museum of history or grave of the past, exists in consistent reality beneath epitaphs of fate that witness to museum woman, museum man, museum landlord, museum peasant, museum revolution. The militancy of the past in overturning the future makes for an inverse and sinisterly comic *avant-garde* fiction in contradistinction to fashionable expectations: *avante-garde* fiction is expected progressively to demolish the past in the present that becomes obsolete in its turn as the future becomes the new, militant, dogmatic present.

By turning the linear thrust of the *avant-garde* towards a museum of history, by inscribing into the past a militancy normally reserved for the present and future, twentieth-century fiction lays itself open to a philosophic humour that is intuitively active, I find, in *Pedro Páramo*. The solid, protuberant present and implicitly the solid, protuberant future are not absolutely demolished as the past would be by a progressive, forward-flowing *avant-garde* function. Instead, present and future connexions and contradictions cohere paradoxically in the past, towards which they flow backward in comedy of psychical time. The change in protuberant cloak that occurs is qualitative, to make room for the aerial nemesis that evokes a sensation of mental responsibility, comedy of psyche, as the properties of the present and future are uplifted and borne by the limbs of ghosts. Thus quantitative design, quantitative realism, mutates into mental or psychical gravity. (See also Chapter Three where we commented upon comedy of parable in Toomer's new-world Christ who "walks upon the waters where huge bubbles burst.")

The philosophic humour that exists at the heart of backward-flowing stream-of-consciousness bears upon *avant-garde* linear progression to suggest, I would say, that the militancy of a forward-flowing stream that lives in dread loathing of the brute legacies of the past may also unthinkingly or mechanically overturn the future and create a void in human responsibility for events past, present or to come. Each mindless preservation, or mindless demolition, what is mindlessly preserved or mindlessly swept away, changes nothing in terms of creative understanding or human profundity.

The arousal of the mental traveller is the beginning of a conversion of robot linearity into revolutionary curvature/revolving cycle upon which ghosts of infinity appear to suffer elemental or aerial responsibility for civilisation and to touch subconsciously/unconsciously, in Rulfo's case, a 'point' akin to unborn living. It is as if buried in the ghost of infinity lies not only the aerial, elemental dead but also the unborn living or twin spirit of the future. In Rulfo's case, that spirit is imbued with great bleakness *in the form of nemesis or mental purgatory*, but even so, it touches upon the conversion of linear deprivation or quantitative fate into qualitative insight or energy or innovative genius.

The ground of mental travel in *Voss* differs markedly from the bleak nemesis that *Pedro Páramo* exhibits in the soil of modern/ancient Mexico. The realist texture of *Voss* tends to give a common sense vision to events and it is largely by way of fantasy that a disruption is created in the apparatus of so-called realism to expose, if not bleak nemesis then the bite of history, in the debasement of Aboriginal peoples, the sense of uniform pigmentation and parentage of society in the wake of immigration policies biased towards whites. That bite, or approximation towards Mexican nemesis, in Patrick White's realism, imbues *Voss* with its curiously subversive fantasy. A *hiatus* or gulf is planted by such fantasy in uniform parent or institution. The strength of such parent, reinforced by codes of naturalism, *is* a feature of nemesis after all and of unconscious degrees by which a society is ordered into acceptance of a parent institution that hardens into the shadowless hubris Voss harnesses into himself and onto his expedition into the future of a continent. But that future begins to lean simultaneously, confusedly, upon the cast-off double or shadow to fertilise itself in an endangered body, endangered womb of space, endangered arts of community.

The parallels that run through *Pedro Páramo* and *Voss* do not entirely bridge the gulf between realism and fantasy that exists within the structure of *Voss*. Yet they do assist us to appreciate the originality of White's strange novel. They do assist us to perceive *realism and fantasy* as a threshold into *evolution and alchemy*. That threshold is a component of the 'mental bridge' within and across cultures that we have been exploring. Now it becomes necessary, before we resume the exploration of *Voss*, to re-consider briefly *variables of fantasy/rainbow bridge* that already exist in the 'womb of space' through *Invisible Man* (Chapter Three) and *Pym* (Chapter Two).

In *Pym*, we confronted the rainbow arc or bridge that inevitably breaks to convey the paradox of creation in both the heights, above the bridge, and in the depths beneath the bridge. In *Invisible Man*, we confronted the seal that imprisons mutuality, kills ecstasy and leaves in its train *a blind contract and broken bridge* into daylight reconnaissance. Trueblood's incest with Matty Lou was mirrored in a dream, in the lightning flash of spontaneous flying carnival *that failed to bridge the divide in humanity* that consolidates itself into incestuous block or hardened institution to encompass the economics of narcissistic ego.

A prime component in invisible man's bridge across or through concentric horizons is the 'descent of the stone' that cultivates those horizons. That 'stone' is also an aspect of mutated or evolved, yet solid, realistic body that invisible man protests he possesses when the novel commences. At the heart of the bridge that Ellison builds lies, therefore, the shadow of mental imagery in which 'solid body' *evolves* into 'stone' in a 'psychical pool' and then *alchemises* further into inner construction across the gulf between a solid, realistic, yet invisible and frustrated body (on one hand) and fantasy, rainbow arc or potential visualisation of newborn/unborn community (on the other).

It is a bridge that remains suspended but available to the cross-cultural innovative imagination. It is a bridge whose construction touches upon the alchemisation of the elements, relics of stone that convert into immaterial fire (as in *Wide Sargasso Sea* and in *The Chosen Place, the Timeless People*). It is a relic or corpse that evolves in Faulkner's "sending of the dead" into a threshold across cultures as into therapeutic *hungan*.

An art that subsists on *evolution and alchemy* acquires a concreteness of vision in its multi-pigmented arc that runs deeper and also wider than the scope of a realism that seems both naturally fated and blind to the mystery of reality. It incurs at times a terrifying weight and weightlessness to reflect a measure of human spirit of responsibility in the shock of past and future events. Alchemisation of elements may appear anthropomorphic, but its impulse is towards an exposure of partial natures that masquerade as a universe of total fact. Considerable concentration is required to descend and to arise within sensual limits that cannot be bypassed, which as a consequence may invoke nemesis or despair but which, by the same token, may pitch the imagination so deep that it gains a configuration of the heights within the pressure of the depths to achieve the actuality of perpetual discovery, of endlessly discoverable peaks of emotion in the arts of freedom and passion for truth.

Evolution is a suspect term in the vocabulary of a major critic such as T. S. Eliot and later in this study I shall return to Eliot's strictures through his reflections on Pascal. I shall also look closely in the last phase of this chapter at the consequences of non-evolutionary datum in Hindu creativity through a celebrated twentieth-century Indian novel by Raja Rao.

My own passion in favour of evolution is clear: I use the term in a profoundly cultural and variable sense to imply that though the million-year-old psyche of humanity appears to be changeless in essence, it would be folly to identify what is virtually an unfathomable 'point of being' with any rigid parent or total investiture in cultural terms. Such total and enlarged identification of the measureless 'point of humanity' in a cosmic creation encourages parochial blindness and disease, it tilts the harlequin animal which Man is into the Voodoo arms of the "sent [institutionalised] dead."

I also use the term evolution to imply a variable bridge not only between human cultures and animal cultures in a biologic and geologic sense, but between human cultures and human cultures, multi-faceted, multi-dimensional, heterogeneous. In that variable bridge arises the conception of alchemy as dialogue of grace between the heights and the depths, in which each variable bridge dissolves to reappear. C. G. Jung points out that in his researches into alchemy, the work of alchemy, however well-intentioned, however arduous, requires the intervention or mystery of grace if it is to be fulfilled. This notion seems to me invaluable if we are to begin to rid ourselves of the appetite for conquest and for the rejection of others as illusory bodies conscripted by fanatical codes and persuasions. The illumination of partial evolution—the conversion of mutated legacies and blind organs—is peculiarly available to the mind of art within a dialogue with otherness, and the basis of that dialogue between one and other, between the heights and the depths, has its 'immeasurable point' in acceptance of the mystery of grace ceaselessly *within* yet ceaselessly *without* human and natural endeavours.

It is an assertion of timeless potentiality without bypassing the pressure of limits, the miracle of individual freedom, the painful yet sometimes ecstatic immersion in, conversion of, deprived order.

That paradox—immersion in, conversion of, limits—brings us back to the gulf between realism and fantasy that we observed in *Voss*, and to the original play of shadow that illumines the thrust of the novel towards the *alchemisation of hubris*.

The partial interchange of lives, between Laura Trevelyan and her emancipist servant Rose Portion, comes to a climax when Rose Portion dies giving birth to the child who is named Mercy Trevelyan, yet is of "unexplained origin" as Voss's symbolic paternity fades into Laura's 'widowhood' and grief. "She succeeded in drawing a shroud about herself."[12] It is a *living* shroud that matches, as we shall see, the *living* epitaph in the person of the "ticket-of-leave" ex-convict Judd, whom Voss recruits into his doomed expedition. Judd becomes "the strength of silence" but supports other features and faces, and bewildered, contradictory voices, that break his silence when, as the sole survivor of the expedition, he returns to civilisation. Thus the shadow of Jack Slipper falls before the expedition commences and the shadow of Judd falls when it ceases. The partial interchange of lives between Laura and Rose is reflected in the allegorical and religious bond between Voss and Judd, which appears when Voss recruits Judd into the expedition.

Voss approaches Judd's farm with its sheep and lambs. He is "jubilant as brass. Cymbals clapped drunkenly. Now he had forgotten words but sang his jubilation in a cracked bass, that would not have disgraced temples, because dedicated to God. Yes. GOTT. He had remembered. He had sung it. It rang out, shatteringly, like a trumpet blast. Even the depths lead upward to that throne, meandered his inspired thoughts. He straightened his shoulders, lying back along the croup of the crazily descending horse . . . he accepted his own divinity. . . ." He recalled the voice of Laura as she worshipped him and "wrestled with him in the garden."[13]

Voss's jubilant arrogation of divinity to himself is linked into Judd's "lambs' blood" reflected in a pool of sky, a pooled constellation of shadowed faces in a basin of water. When Voss arrives at Judd's farm, Judd "purposely led his guest to a cleft where a spring welled into a basin of amber water. Black, rocky masses, green, skeleton ferns, the pale features of men, all fluctuated in the mirror of water. Taking off his shirt, Judd got upon his knees and was washing off the lambs' blood with a piece of crude soap already there on a rock ledge. He is strong, mused Voss, considering not so much the thick body as some strength of silence of which the man was possessed."[14]

The crudity of baptism is appropriate to the self-mocking difficulty of establishing a dialogue between the heights and the depths when the heights have been pre-empted by Voss's hubris and the depths fluctuate with "pale features of men" standing upon Judd's half-reflected trunk that is invested with the "strength of silence." What White does not strictly intend but is nevertheless active intuition within cross-cultural and 'alchemised stone' that we are pursuing in the womb of historical/fictional space, is that the marriage of jubilation and silence in Voss and Judd spells the curious *living* epitaph of the expedition that Judd is to become, and the painful descent Voss is to make from his egocentric saddle of god-man fate into the grave of doomed expedition under a rainbow bridge of stars. In *Voss* we may intuit, therefore, within alchemised stone, 'the death of god/the death of Man' in crude parallels of Vossian hubris and Juddian shadow. For in Judd we begin to perceive the destined homecoming of living epitaph to Voss's 'widow' Laura, who is indebted to Jack Slipper and Rose Portion.

Judd is oblivious of the part he is destined to play. He is a pawn and remains a pawn when he returns, a disorientated survivor, to civilisation. His disorientation is of the unconscious folk, folk spirit, imprisoned in space.

The disorientation began long before. It begins on the first symbolic day he meets hubristic Voss and is possessed by the other's intransigent, epic stature, so that he stares backward as well as forward into antecedents and progeny of non-memory within the spring from which he has washed the "lambs' blood."

Judd is reminiscent of invisible man. "Circles expanding on the precious water made it seem possible that this was the centre of the earth."[15] It is the centre, yet it is also the expanding cycle of the whirling stone we have been pursuing through alchemies of water and fire, incest, debased carnival women, bull's blood, Icarus/ Anancy, reeling earth that takes Voss's bones out of Laura's grasp in the garden where they consummate an unfulfilled union of past and future, unfulfilled conversion of interior spring or pool into possessions of earth and sky.

The living epitaph of Judd within Voss's "drunken cymbals" is woven into the pool of space to come to ceaselessly fluctuating head or features of imperilled humanity. As living epitaph, he embodies vacancies of memory and tells contradictory tales on his return to civilisation.

Religious crisis is documentary crisis, it is a crisis of memory, as Judd's living epitaph of humanity, like Juan Preciado's backward-flowing spectre, implies. In other words, one may say that the ground of religious crisis in *Voss* establishes the peculiar distance White's 'invisible man', Judd, has travelled in history toward circular memory or non-memory that taxes originality.

How are we to apportion that tax within Vossian/Juddian legacies? Mercy, we may recall, is Voss's and Laura's 'daughter', though the roots of fable have long faded over the years with

Laura's 'widowhood' and grief, and Mercy is taxed by her adoptive
mother's acute distress after the conversation her mother has had
with ex-convict Judd.

Mercy Trevelyan absorbs something of the price of symbolic
marriage, something of Laura's obsessed attachment to epic model
in Voss that has engendered cultural amnesia and embarrassment
on another level of suppressed code in respect to Rose Portion's
lover, Jack Slipper. Jack, the harlequin journeyman, is related to
Voss, as already noted, as inverse pawn to epic hero or leader of
the expedition. These are all variations upon the shadow-fertility-
tax that Mercy and Laura bear across the generations in
conjunction with "mad" Judd and the contradictory tales he tells of
god-man Voss's life and death.

The truths of epic run far deeper and stranger than complacent
order or respectable document or prime minister or president or
enshrined ancestor of state.

The intricate link between hubristic lover, Voss, and shadow
lover, Jack, cannot escape us. For ironically it is Voss who forfeits
and Jack, the shadow, who gains fleshly intercourse with Rose to
illumine other horizons of memory and non-memory within
sophistications and patchwork titles shared by so-called
distinguished members of society, by Colonel Hebden, by old Mr
Sanderson, and by other stalwarts of the so-called enlightened
historic day in whose circle Laura moves like a sleepwalker.

Such horizons of memory and non-memory are motifs of the
harlequin body of a new society in which amnesia and
embarrassment tend to polarise origins and to solidify deception
into moral imperative. Thus hubris in one shape or another
masquerades as moral authority. The painful fissuring of one-
sided, moral ground—the alchemisation of hubris—begins to
shadow Voss as he journeys deeper and deeper into Aboriginal
dream-time as into a congregation of souls who fly upward like silk
into "whirling circles of blue sky." Voss learns of these "whirling
circles" from a black Aboriginal in his party when they come upon
a "tree platform" designed for the "migration of aboriginal souls."[16]

That platform is Aboriginal cousin to the living epitaph Judd is
destined to become. It bears upon memory and eclipsed memory's
whirling circles into which the re-born dead fly—immortal geese,

divine manuscript, aerial silk, all tokens of esoteric evolution. One is reminded of *Invisible Man* and Trueblood's naive, thwarted ecstasy despite his fleeting vision of "flying geese" before he falls back into incestuous code or illiterate blindness on the bed he shares with his wife and daughter.

The living epitaph of Aboriginal cousin and disoriented Judd reaches into cosmic alphabet to overshadow Voss before he is beheaded by the Aboriginals. He witnesses, in the week preceding his death, the Rainbow Serpent that writes itself with stars in the sky. This is a confusing apparition that sows distress amongst the Aboriginals themselves. They had been told of it by their elders but had long dismissed it as a fable with each passing generation that conformed, it seemed, to levels of tamed cosmos. "All their lives haunted by spirits, these had been of a colourless, invisible, and comparatively amiable variety. Even the freakish spirits of darkness behaved within the bounds of a certain convention. Now this great fiery one came, and threatened the small souls of men. . . ."[17]

The appearance of the great comet or Rainbow Serpent coincides with the arrival of Voss, Judd and the white men in their party from another world. It is an occasion for heart-searching distress amongst the Aboriginals whose "small souls" are baffled by the extremity of space into which the "tree-platform" extends itself. "Through the chinks in the very black twigs, blue was poured into blue, until there was no measuring its depths. Sparks were flying, or stars. . . ." So here at last, in confirmation of incredible legend, had come "the Great Snake, the grandfather of all men . . . come down from the north in anger."[18]

The emphasis on anger reveals the confusion and rage with which the Aboriginals view the arrival of Voss and his party in the shadow of a rain of stars that runs curiously parallel to Caribbean Arawak/Macusi creation myth and the sky of fiction in which mad Bertha of *Jane Eyre* is re-dressed into Jean Rhys's intensely yearning, intensely human Antoinette upon "her tree of fire . . . in flames."

Thus we may see the death of Voss as consistent with creation myth rooted in the necessity for community to evolve through complex visions of apparent catastrophe. The conception of a "doubling star" (though the tone in *Voss* read against the tone in *Wide Sargasso Sea* varies profoundly) applies as much to Voss as to mad Bertha/Antoinette. Whereas Bertha was reputed to be mad, Voss has arrogated to himself the hubris of divinity and it is this schizophrenia, this implicit obsession with conquest, that turns upon him in the sky of the Aboriginal Serpent: the blood in his veins may seek to erect itself into a flag in the stars but a price has to be paid for such idolatry.

Voss is as vulnerable as they are, the black Aboriginals discover, when they make an incision in his flesh. The drop of blood that stains the finger of one man who makes the fissure or cut vanishes so quickly it leaves no mark to show to the others, who are nevertheless convinced, it would seem, of the invisible stain or depth of shadow that breaches idolatry to sow the stars in heaven. An unconscious irony arises here. It is perfectly feasible to relate consensus—about the "colourless, invisible, within the bounds of convention."[19] Their loss of faith in Voss then becomes a further manifestation of their own tamed vision.

On the other hand, as I have implied, they may have perceived *the alchemisation of hubris* as the lesson of untamable Serpent ancestor, in communion with the broken body of the white invader, whose shadow of blood adds an invisible cut or stitch to a backcloth of stars.

The subtle cut or fissure of hubris is there in *Voss*, it is startlingly original in obscure essence and profound fantasy; yet the white man's documentation of Aboriginal superstitious response to the Rainbow Serpent eclipses creativity between invader and invaded. The wealth of fertile alliance in the encounter of cultures tends to become a statistic of so-called savage mind and to fade; even as the spectre of Voss's mystical paternity of Mercy Trevelyan tends to fade in Laura's mind and to awaken only a little, if at all, in the encounter with ex-convict Judd and "ticket-of-leave lambs' blood."

The Aboriginals' incision into Voss's dying flesh fades into a mere document stored in a museum of fictions to confirm a state of endemic callousness. The collapse of an expedition in the mid-nineteenth century becomes but a momentary set-back in the funeral of conquest, in conquistadorial and formidably 'progressive' civilisation. How oblivious are victor and victim, so-called civilised Man and so-called Aboriginal, to the enigma of living epitaph and tax upon originality?

The Serpent and the Rope

An important clue, in my judgement, to much twentieth-century Indian literature may lie in variable combinations of Western historical consciousness and non-evolutionary Indian stasis. Perhaps the most remarkable and profoundly intelligent example of this arises in Raja Rao's *The Serpent and the Rope* which appeared in 1960.[20] For there the protagonist Rama plays with the ascendancy of stasis over historical model and the illusory constitution of historical realities upon a non-evolutionary datum of absolutes, absolute Non-Dual Ego, absolute order.

Raja Rao's *The Serpent and the Rope* mirrors a civilisation whose symbols of illusion and reality in the twentieth century may resemble the despair of the West, the despair of history, but are not simply a form of despair since they are rooted, one senses, in a consensus of 'timeless order of mind'. Whatever the corruption and squalor of the India that lies within and behind *The Serpent and the Rope*, the novel cultivates an immunity to indictment by Western models of observation and history when those models themselves—despite the bleak lessons of empires, of depressions, of World Wars—are unlikely to surrender their economic biases in the face of human misery.

Rao's India may therefore embrace the despair of the West but in order to parody the paralysis of history, it would seem, within a bureaucratic orphanage of spirit that divorces itself from parent institutions and from conceptions of evolutionary marriage between cultures and peoples. Such a divorce may appear again to resemble the intractable and divided sovereign institutions of the West but would seem to be different. An assertion of *illusory* descent from age-old parent institutions leads, in Rao's fiction, to *contrived code or child* descended from a marriage of 'ancient refinement and ancient unselfconsciousness'. Thus the child is, in reality, an *orphan of eternity or of absolute Non-Dual Ego*. "I was born an orphan, and have remained one."[21]

The institution of "born orphan" in *The Serpent and the Rope* is clearly not a device to arouse guilt in parent worlds, in the womb of cultural space; it is a device to seal those worlds away forever within *contrivances* of pain and sorrow or guilt that one may still cultivate, if one wishes, as an illusion to offset the creative disruption, the creative disorder, as it were, of genuine transition into alchemised properties of hubris.

The ways in which the novel contrives sorrow, pain, guilt, duty, are of great interest because while they may seem to reflect despair in Western terms, their real function is to confront the apparently suffering Orphan or Ego with a reflection in the mirror of society that is never truly himself. It is an illusion of the sick or the well, the ugly or the beautiful, the rich or the poor. All appearances of suffering are that illusion of deceptive duality between 'one' and 'one's suffering counterpart', and it breeds in self-pity an emotion of the pathos of time.

All appearances, so to speak, are distortions of non-evolutionary identity and as such may only serve to *release* the powerless actor from the tyranny of action when such action brings not mastery of, but repetitive servitude to, pain, violence, poverty. *Release* is too strong a word. Rather one should say that those meaningless distortions, or reflections of Non-Dual Ego, cultivate patterns of consent, consenting public, consenting governed, consenting governors, within elaborate and contrived dialogues with sorrow, beauty or pain. (They are meaningless distortions in that they never imply meaningful fissures to beauty or pain within an asymmetric art that converts emotion into insights of complexly real otherness.)

At the heart of such contrivances lies, therefore, a seductive passivity, an assertion of impossible goals, impossible change, by which one may be deceived into faith in innovative arts of truth, innovative dialogue between past and future within the orphan of the world. That the orphan Rama does succumb to such duality and such pretences of art makes him an unconscious harlequin, I think, since otherwise there would be no novel for Raja Rao to write. That the orphan bleeds in the mirror of family deprivations, that he is stricken by pain, gives to the contrivance a powerful conceit that serves to affirm the absurdity of allegiances that are in essence rituals of self-pity and the incorrigible pathos of time.

The orphan Rama declares—"I was born a Brahmin . . . devoted to Truth and all that. . . . I read the Upanishads at the age of four, was given the holy thread at seven—because my mother was dead and I had to perform the funeral ceremonies, year after year—my father having married again. So with wet cloth and an empty stomach, with devotion, and sandal paste on my forehead, I fell before the rice-bowls of my mother and I sobbed. I was born an orphan, and have remained one. I have wandered the world and have sobbed in hotel rooms and in trains."[22]

It is in the context of profoundly contrived harlequin, which seems to border on unconscious duality, that Rama's pursuit of his mother turns into obsession. The tireless pace of such obsession, in the making of a long and elaborate fiction with which to drape the stases of India-in-Europe-in-Serpent-and-Rope-womb or theatre of space, refuses, whatever Raja Rao's fixed intentions, to accommodate itself absolutely to the negation of duality or to unselfconscious endorsement of a monolith of truth. Thus an element of shrewdly contrived or genuine rebellion (the humour of rebellion) appears in the motley illnesses, the motley spaces, of Non-Dual Ego.

They say my mother was very beautiful and very holy. Grandfather Kittana said, "Her voice, son, was like a *vina* playing to itself, after an evensong is over. . . . It resonated from the depths, from unknown space, and one felt God shone the brighter with this worship. She reminded me of concubine Chandramma."[23]

God in Hindu theology is not Other. God pre-empts all selves within absolute Non-Dual Ego. Thus "brighter worship" is required as pre-emptive reflection into the Ego's "unknown space(s)" which are constantly at risk in a motley firmament or mirror of suspended otherness that threatens the holy Ego by infusing it with fears, lusts and biases to undermine pre-emptive reflection, pre-emptive subjection of all natures in concubinage to the Ego.

Indeed "holy mother/concubine goddess" endorses the threat of motley firmament or sky of illness that runs into unknown spaces within the Ego of the cosmos; for these "unknown spaces" are pregnant with continuing obsession for impossible union between the mother of beauty and beauty's orphaned reflection. The obsession is so strong that space is as much the Ego's realm as a source of motley and half-rebellious legend. Such motley or

unconscious harlequin aids and abets legends that Rama tells of the
winged horse/mutual tiger that may well have soared "into the sky
of India."[24] That flight is an occasion for wonder and surprise, and
yet it is no surprise. Genuine astonishment or wonder would be a
confession of real activity, real partiality within and without the
Ego, whereas flying horse or tiger is ritualised, ironically stultified
carnival within a medium of changeless gravity or suspended
intercourse between the heights and the depths.

All in all, a grain of dark rebellious humour in harlequin or
motley sky is alive in Rama. The stultification of active intercourse
between the heights and the depths becomes weighted with the
irony of mediating Narcissus (the strangest eccentricity of Absolute
Ego and Suspended Other). Changeless order changes into both
progeny of legend and parent of legend, *it is stained by mental
incest*. It becomes an indelible harlequin addiction to shades of
beauty and grief that settle over the body of the narrative and give
it a sensation of archaic modernity, archaic rebellion. The posture
of 'timeless order'—compounded of fascinating contrivance,
genuine obsession, eccentric Narcissus—makes *The Serpent and
the Rope*, I find, a profoundly revealing, confessional fiction of
conservative South India. Equally fascinating is the degree in which
it resembles European despair and philosophies of the absurdity of
mutual existences or genuine wealth in reciprocity between
cultures.

The obsession with threatening "concubine/holy mother" or
with absurd "flying horse/tiger/grandfather" is a play on "Truth
and all that." "All that" becomes the incorrigible appetite of multi-
reflecting harlequin who subsists on the sickness of his age but
resolutely voids the possibility of converting that sickness into
anything other than illusory marriage to illusory otherness. As a
consequence, the conception of psychical re-dress leading into
economic or cultural metamorphosis (to which we have addressed
ourselves as intuitively available to previous fictions) does not arise
in *The Serpent and the Rope* to affect the language of the novel;
that language remains uniformly a blend of historical narrative and
subtle mock-epic which—Indian critics claim—is imbued by
Sanskrit rhythms.

The shift from mother India to bride of Europe (when Rama

marries a Frenchwoman called Madeleine) takes the orphan of space through a series of refinements of despair in his neurosis of paradisaical affection.

Rama seeks a paraphrase for that neurosis in mock-epic, mock-allegoric history and in Dantesque and Hitlerian parallels, impossible (ideal) tyrant Beatrice and terrifying "real" Eva Braun.

Beatrice, O Beatrice is beautiful in Paradise. But what an impossible tyrant she becomes . . . She who should see the light through [Dante], now wants to show the light to him. *It is the inversion of Truth.* Where the world cannot annihilate itself . . . it has to make itself feminine. . . . Buddhism went to Tibet, and gave itself many paradises. Tantra entered Hinduism, and worshipping the women, made the world real. Man became thus the everlasting, the superman, the slave of himself, and all such supermen must end in the stink . . . of a dug-out. Eva Braun showed the world was real. The ogre, the superman Hitler . . . died. . . . The miracle must for ever end in emptiness.

The "inversion of [the] Truth"—in Rama's paraphrase—resembles the debased faculty of the muse that we have been tracing in previous chapters but—in its own philosophical terms—it is not debasement but impossible goal that is intended, impossible muse-factor, impossible *coniunctio* between sexes and cultures. For true *coniunctio* would imply that both are partial in dual reality and neither should seek to pre-empt the other into a stasis of Non-Dual Ego. The impossibility of true *coniunctio* in the philosophical apparatus of *The Serpent and the Rope* has no alternative therefore but to mirror regressed ideal rather than evolved community, degraded—rather than alchemised—hubris in the superman who is the everlasting "slave of himself" in worshipping women. His stinking dug-out is the "real" world he has erroneously created within the evil of duality by which he is possessed, paradise after paradise, conquest after conquest.

The miracle that must for ever end in emptiness is impossible love, impossible otherness, impossible wings, impossible Beatrice on "grandfather's winged horse or tiger" at the door of "unknown spaces," motley paradises.

When Rama and Madeleine part company, it is less the gentle and plagued Madeleine whom the orphan of space mourns (since she is eternally widowed in the arms of his mother) and more, much more, burden of obsessed "Truth and all that," which now genuinely afflicts him, and in which he cannot rid himself of Beatrice, the mother of allegory, who appears to have no recourse but to regress into Eva Braun's consenting posture to real horror, to the rape of a civilisation that she has come helplessly and unwittingly to symbolise within an age of concubine politics.

Rama's mausoleum of history gives him away by degrees of obsession with the making of a fiction that lives. *The Serpent and the Rope* lives as an imaginative achievement. Its obsessions have bred not only motley euphemisms and holy concubines, but genuine remorse and misgiving, if not the torment of the damned. At times it seems almost to turn into sly tongue-in-cheek comedy. Is idolised Woman who turns the tables on Man—on epic poet as on superman—an authoritarian joke upon pre-emptive, male, ritual womb? One cannot really say. The answer seems to suspend itself in male and female *personae*, who regress into interchangeable ciphers of tyranny in a world as pre-ordained for bureaucratic orphanage of spirit as it is for psychical widowhood in a helpless succession of illusory bodies and generations.

SIX

Harlequin and Psyche

Discontinuity, Decadence and Innovation

The emphasis I have placed on alchemies of evolution needs to be judged, as we have seen, against contrary as well as variable conceptions. *The Serpent and the Rope*, despite its addiction to non-evolutionary datum, has assisted in terms of cross-cultural perspective to deepen our inquiry into the games or masquerades men and women may be conscripted to play by the Non-Dual Ego. That conscription invests in absolute continuity of an institutional mask seeking to cement together all orders of being into a reality that annihilates dialogue, whatever contrivances of dialogue it may maintain as the stuff of illusion. The danger here has been curiously, perhaps involuntarily, depicted by T. S. Eliot in an essay on the 'Pensées' of Pascal. Eliot concludes his essay on the 'Pensées' with the following remarks.

We cannot quite understand any of the parts, fragmentary as they are, without some understanding of the whole. Capital, for instance, is [Pascal's] analysis of the *three orders*: the order of nature, the order of mind, the order of charity. These three are *discontinuous*; the higher is not implicit in the lower as in an evolutionary doctrine it would be. In this distinction Pascal offers much about which the modern world would do well to think. . . . I can think of no Christian writer, not Newman even, more to be commended than Pascal to those who doubt, but who have the mind to conceive, and the sensibility to feel, the disorder, the futility, the meaninglessness, the mystery of life and suffering, and who can only find peace through a satisfaction of the whole being.[1]

The discontinuity of which Eliot speaks, in league with his rebuttal of "evolutionary doctrine," yields a profound ambiguity in my judgement. It is *the alchemisation of, or paradoxes of vision into, evolutionary layers blind in themselves,* that one needs to turn and face in inmost self-reflection. That alchemisation subtly disrupts the carapace or code within the miraculously perceiving self, miraculously perceptive human animal. That very alchemisation makes for discontinuity within territorial imperatives—within 'totalitarian' models of instinct—that begin, therefore, to mutate in the depths, even as they open themselves to the heights, and to innovative dialogue amongst parts of an unfathomable whole.

Thus, the higher may *not* be "implicit in the lower" as strict formula or tamed identity, but it is susceptible to itself as a part of unfathomable cosmos *through* the miracle of human perception that seeks to translate/re-dress all codes into fractions and factors of truth. That re-dress of the higher in the lower and vice versa is a fissure in *personae* of conquest which so often masquerade as divine or higher moral authorities.

It would be folly to disguise from ourselves the problematic idea of one-sided order that obsesses many major Western thinkers, artists and poets. That is, the tendency we have seen elaborated in Poe, for example, to maintain a fixture of block commander even as his schizophrenic genius asserts the partiality of all institutions, the discontinuity within realms of being, and the death-wish that block commander implies unless it cannibalises its biases, in some potent or renascent degree, that opens a door upon transubstantial grace, transubstantial innovation.

This dilemma, in my judgement, is at the heart of the twentieth-century European and American novel, whether it calls itself *avant-garde* or otherwise. In parallel with it is the growing tendency to opt for contrivances to feed the mass-media.

There is a growing market for violence and for varieties of sophisticated and crude obscenity. Novels are discussed by the pundits of television and press as if they are junk food to be consumed in an instant as a 'good read'. What is a 'good read', in this context, if not a sex-consumer euphemism, four-letter words upon the dust jacket of culture?

Despite, or even because of, this, there are separate spirits whose solitary neurosis of genius encapsules the dilemmas of community and "offers [in Eliot's phrase about Pascal] much about which the modern world would do well to think." An outstanding example is the novel *Gormenghast* by the English writer and artist Mervyn Peake.[2]

Gormenghast was first published in 1950 in London, three years after the appearance of Ellison's *Invisible Man* in the United States and seven years or so before White's Australian *Voss* was published in Britain.

In its extremity, the novel possesses a certain kinship to ironies of "discontinuous order," in the Eliotesque sense, that we perceive in *Voss* and *Invisible Man*. The discontinuity in *Voss* is particularly marked first with Voss and Judd, second with Laura and Rose Portion. There is an *order of mind* in Voss, an *order of nature* in Judd and Rose Portion, an *order of charity* in Laura and in Rose Portion's child, Mercy, whom Laura adopts. One needs however to make a significant qualification with respect to these orders.

Voss's order of mind possesses a certain resistance to evolutionary change and tends therefore to clothe itself in a growing death-wish, in a monolithic hubris; that hubris imprisons the order of nature in Judd and Rose Portion, so that the necessity for innovative dialogue between convicted nature and hubristic mind becomes acute in Judd's fragmentary memories of expedition into the heartland. Judd's half-human, half-divine (as well as half-animal, half-social) madness is a buried component in Voss's mind as well that needs to be released before it deprives Laura's Mercy of *creative* love between the animal nature of Rose, from which Mercy comes, and the psychical motherhood of Laura, in which Mercy finds shelter.

The discontinuity in *Invisible Man* may be traced, in some degree, within a capacity for epic, nameless parts through which may be approached the gestation of unseen, yet existing, foetal humanity in the womb of space. That epic gestation possesses its fugitive dreaming mind (black Anancy-Nobody-Odysseus in a Cyclopean cave of the womb), its fugitive dreaming nature (paradoxes of surreal, incestuous Trueblood), its fugitive charity (compensation bestowed by the paint factory in the wake of explosive dream-dismemberment).

The buried components of half-animal, half-social Judd and Rose Portion in Voss's and Laura's unconscious mind run parallel, in some degree, to fugitive dreaming mind/fugitive dreaming charity in invisible man's odyssey. One could say, for example, that the child Mercy in *Voss* remains overshadowed by a gestating body of community in which fugitive orders of being witness to an emergency, to a phenomenon of birth akin nevertheless to foetal, non-evolutionary status or non-birth. Without those fugitive orders (mind, nature, charity), no emergency would exist; the death of the human species would be confirmed as realistically normal however mechanically alive humankind appears to be in the museum of the womb. And such mechanics of life would confirm an ape of soul or signal of inner demise. It is this terrifying anguish, this tension between fugitive orders and museum of the womb, that gives *Gormenghast* its spectral colour and neurosis of genius.

It is a tension that commits itself to the funeral of a civilisation, but makes a formidable occasion of that funeral, so formidable one is drawn into a sensation of living blood on a canvas of dreams within the mind of a child, whose ironies of Trueblood descent lead him to marshal a body of ghosts and shades—ambiguities of the "quick and the dead"—in a "little revolution" against the 'death of Man'.[3]

Titus is seven. . . . He is *child*. The gift of the bright blood. Of blood that laughs. . . . Of blood that mourns. . . . O little revolution in great shades. Titus the Seventy-Seventh. Heir to a crumbling summit: . . . Gormenghast. . . . Is all corroding? No. Through an avenue of spires a zephyr floats; a bird whistles; . . . *And darkness winds between the characters.* Who are the characters? . . . Tall figures bow. Some in jewelry; some in rags.[4]

Titus's "little revolution" leads him into Gormenghast's "library and its ashes." Here he encounters in the womb of Gormenghast space, an ancestral, fugitive order of mind "armored with learning, with philosophy, with poetry that drifts or dances, clamped though it is in midnight. . . . Cold weight of ink, . . . the ghost of Sepulchrave. . . ."[5]

This encounter with his predecessor, with "weight of ink," is the fossil, midnight blood of dreams into which he dips his pen in the school of Gormenghast.[6] "He saw the glass marble beside the inkpot, with its swirling spirals of rainbow colours. . . . It was wealth. . . . How it could clink and crack like a gunshot when it struck another! . . . Oh, blood-alleys!"[7]

The varied architectonic canvas and tone of the narrative cannot but remind one of the pre-Columbian rainbow bridge and tree, linking sky and earth as well as arching across spaces, as discussed in Chapters Two and Three. It is fruitful, I find, to visualise Titus's "little revolution in great shades" subsisting upon spirals of the rainbow within which he encounters "marshaled ghosts."[8] Beneath the rainbow bridge (or rainbow tree) is the "cruel water of night" upon which Gormenghast floats and appears rooted at times in swirls and spirals: "Through an avenue of spires a zephyr floats."[9] The pressure of museum space upon the child Titus to alchemise the stony-hearted, yet floating Gormenghast, into a living fossil of weird adventure and comedy becomes the source of doubled, and re-doubled elaborate costumes and masks that the characters wear as darkness winds between them.

Bellgrove sleeps. Dogseye carves. Flay is the Long Man of the Woods. Steerpike is a subversive demon who burns and plots. Sourdust is succeeded as Master of Ritual by his aged son Barquentine. "Abiatha Swelter wades in a sluglike illness of fat through the humid ground mists of the Great Kitchen."[10]

Titus's rainbow possesses its majestic marble of beauty that "sears a skein of cloud," with which he fells his enemies within "a light too violent for ghosts, and Keda, Sourdust, Flay, Swelter, and Sepulchrave dissolve into sunbeams." Their apparent dissolution and fall, however, is as much his loss or void as theirs. Titus is incomplete without them. They are not just his adversaries but regressed faculties of the mind and the nature of dreams that deprive yet sustain him close to zero pulsation, a thread of capacity in the womb of space, even as he wrestles with them in their unprepossessing metamorphoses into frightful, yet paradoxical (because sometimes innocuous, absurdly playful) monsters. And their fall from the bridge or tree leaves him suddenly exposed to an order of fossil charity, a museum epitaph of love, brought to

him by his mother. "Her love for him is . . . heavy and . . .
formless. . . . A furlong of white cats trails after her. A bullfinch has a nest in her red hair. She is the Countess Gertrude
of huge clay."[11]

Thus Titus's "little revolution in great shades" appears to
succumb before it has well begun to the funeral of an age, but this
terminal fate qualifies or modifies itself. The marriage of dissolving
adversaries and fugitives (Titus's half-intimates, half-servants, of
history) to "a light too violent for ghosts" is an occasion for re-
doubled inspection of animal masks, whether cat or bullfinch or
other apparently natural or mythological creature. It is the live,
untamable blood of art, and the *light*, untamable blood of
darkness, that makes a celebration of mourning, so that the
emphasis upon "revolution" may shift into intuitively rebellious
fossils, into the *life* within an apparent *decadence* of heart and
mind.

One now approaches, I believe, the essential problematic issue
that resides in *Gormenghast*, that of decadence. And we need to
look at the associations this evokes. 'Decadence' has varied in inner
meaning across many generations. Carlyle in his *History of the
French Revolution* approached 'decadence' with a puritan
conviction that led him to declare that there are "those decadent
ages in which no Ideal either grows or blossoms." His judgement
continues to operate wherever decadence is equated with decline or
sterility.

On the other hand, there is a paradox of illuminating cross-
cultures built into so-called decadence. For example, Théophile
Gautier, in a preface to Baudelair's *Fleurs du Mal* in 1868, made the
following observation:

The style inadequately called of decadence is nothing but art arrived at the
point of extreme maturity yielded by the slanting suns of aged
civilisations; an ingenious, complicated style, full of shades and of
research, constantly pushing back the boundaries of speech, borrowing
from all technical vocabularies, taking color from all palettes and notes
from all keyboards, struggling to render what is most inexpressible in
thought, what is vague and most elusive in the outlines of form, listening to
translate the subtle confidences of neurosis, the dying confessions of
passion grown depraved, and the strange hallucinations of the obsession
which is turning to madness.[12]

Gautier brings into extreme focus a view of decadence that expresses undoubted admiration for "complicated style" in which a movement across conventional boundaries occurs, a coincidence of arts, as it were, that takes "color from all palettes and notes from all keyboards," so that a poem or fiction may absorb metaphors that relate to painting or sculpture or organic images of music. And yet uneasiness is all too manifest in Gautier's annunciation of decadence and its addiction to "subtle confidences of neurosis . . . obsession which is turning to madness." This ambiguity, I find, may be traced in the writings of others who admired 'decadence', writers such as Eugene Delacroix, and Baudelaire, who described Wagner's music "as excelling in painting space."[13]

It would seem safe to deduct that Baudelaire was not aware how indebted Wagner was to Beethoven's late quartets and Ninth Symphony, which were not performed, I believe, until long after Beethoven's death, but which were read in manuscript by Wagner. Anton Ehrenzweig recounts Wagner's debt to Beethoven in his critical study, *The Hidden Order of Art*. Wagner, Ehrenzweig explains, created a revolution in music. I mention all this because in the light of such a debt, the question arises: was Beethoven a composer of 'decadence' in stimulating Wagner's alteration of boundaries between 'pure' sound and 'mental' space, painted mind in rhythmic space? What seems to me curiously clear, though unstated within the logic of decadence advanced by Gautier, Delacroix, Baudelaire and others, is that their manifest uneasiness at a conception of art that alters boundaries may stem from symmetries of habit—symmetry built into local, purist order of paint, symmetry build into local, purist order of sound, symmetry built into local, purist order of word. These symmetries were natural, or naturalistic, in the light of the cultural, homogeneous biases that remained formidable in European civilisation despite four centuries of imperial conquest and colonisation around the globe.

Nevertheless, the impact of nightsky cultures within the carapace of conquest, however marginally or peculiarly visible, was becoming part of the European experience of global cross-cultures, and it was to usher in (if I may give three examples that come quickly to mind) Gauguin's dialogue with the Pacific, Picasso's dialogue with the African mask, Henry Moore's dialogue with pre-Columbian sculptures.

The prisonhouse of a logic of symmetric bias, or closed, purist order, so underpinned all such innovative dialogue, that it becomes darkly clear why the term 'decadence' was adopted; in purist logic, decadence was the fruit of fate; it was both "mature" and "mad." It incorporated into itself a new refinement or stoic submission to the consequences of failing conquistadorial empires abroad, and the failing Napoleonic empire at home, it incorporated into itself an ardour for nihilism in the midst of bankrupt orders or a concept of hypocritical, liberal good. The complex parable of the conversion of deprivations—deprivations so often masked by purist orders—was overlooked, it would seem, by philosophies of art, and the judgement of decadence continued into the twentieth century as a refinement of the death-wish, a stoic confrontation with the nemesis of heterogeneity in fugitive, bastard orders of painting, music, poetry and fiction (*bastard* inevitably when seen from the posture of so-called pure yet alienated mind). That the nemesis of heterogeneity inspired admiration nevertheless in Europe was an unconscious tribute to untamable reality, untamable myth.

All this harks back and helps us to re-visualise Eliot's discontinuous orders, which he plucked from Pascal's 'Pensées'—orders of mind, of nature, of charity. These run in their extremity, parallel to 'bastard' order of *fiction* (as, let us say, mind) and poetry, 'bastard' order of *music* (as, let us say, *nature*) and poetry, 'bastard' order of *painting* (as, let us say, *love or charity*) and poetry. I add *poetry* to each category in order to invoke an illegitimate linkage between the three orders, fiction as mind in intercourse with poetry, music as nature in intercourse with poetry, painting as love in intercourse with poetry. The addition of *poetry* also suggests that discontinuity is not the ground of new absolutes but of mixed parents, that it genuinely implies a breakthrough from hoary monoliths, and that therein lies something far subtler and stranger than decadence, something that speaks of innovative genius within the womb of space.

What is at stake, I would suggest, is the difficult uprooting and evolutionary/revolutionary transformation of apparently in-corrigible bias and fear. Such bias and such fear seem concurrent with original evil, original fear; and yet they seem at other times not at all 'original' but offspring of a harlequin cosmos at the heart of existence. That that harlequin cosmos is mixed becomes the irony of despair, the "mature" and the "mad" spirit of decadence that is driven, against its will, to align *bias* with *purity,* and *purity* with the *extermination of others,* and thus to seek the most daring, unbiased annunciation and *coniunctio* of partial mind, partial nature, partial love, within asymmetric and illegitimate infinity of grace—a grace that is utterly astonishing, since it is not the spirit that legend equates with virgin births, virgin origins, virgin legitimacy and so on. The stress of complex re-adjustment in a homogeneous social imperative is very great and age-old virgin hubris may look sullied but dies hard, *and the very moment of re-visioned or potentially recovered* coniunctio *is cast aside almost instantaneously as impure.*

That moment is left to languish as decadence and to subsist upon, or evoke, bitter insecurity until it paints itself with the clamour of heart's blood, heart's peril; the therapy of genesis, as it were, or cosmic, healed parentage (unfathomable male, unfathomable female mystery) succumbs to diseased origin, to conceptions of original violence that holds cultures in thrall.

No wonder decadence and profound originality seem sometimes inextricably woven together. Not only that. Cross-cultural necessity is largely discarded within a logic that is in its essence despair and the consolidation of a death-wish, since the bizarre technologies that marry the elements (atomic, nuclear, etc.) and upon which homogeneous societies subsist, *heighten* the harlequin 'diseased antecedents' of dialectic science, which the puritan mind both needs and fears with such passion that nihilism comes to batten upon purity and to structuralise itself into feud and terrorism from the extreme, 'pure' left and from the extreme, 'pure' right. The latter elect, in all the circumstances, to play at being the biases and purities of God.

The confused nature of origins—original *coniunctio,* original evil—complicates the transformation of dread. Dread comes into equation with incorrigible bias and seeks to banish a true dialogue between mind and nature. Dread seeks a pre-emptive Gorgon-headed strike at love or compassion or charity. Such a pre-emptive strike, one would intuit, is embodied in the fate of Titus's mother, the Countess of Groan or Gertrude of Clay, who masquerades as Gorgon epitaph of love with bullfinch nest in her hair.

In this context, realism *is* the depiction of deprivation, though when it borders upon a sophistication of despair and 'black humour', it is touched by the enigmatic creativity of 'decadence' and may even begin to see itself aligned to paradoxes of nihilism in which a society eclipses the trespass of freedom in order to conscript hard-fisted agents to defend its territorial imperatives, privileges and properties. The intuitive transformation of orders that fossilise into epitaphs brings us back to problematic 'decadence' interwoven with 'pure' realism. It may be of interest, before we return to *Gormenghast,* to sense a very curious parallel between Gertrude of Clay and a character called Fern in the book *Cane* by the American writer Jean Toomer.

Fern, like Muriel of *Box Seat* (see Chapter Three), is a kind of virgin whore of the 1920s though her existence, unlike Muriel's, is marked by many involvements with men to whom she gives herself but remains insensible to contact as if frozen into solid indifference. She is submissive to men (who seek to be healed in her arms) yet she remains so blind and deaf to their inner need of her that she leaves them "baffled and ashamed" as if they stand rebuked in the 'evil' of intercourse.

She incorporates into herself an apparent immobility of feature and landscape. Her eyes mirror still water and tree and land. The "countryside flows" into them. The climax in the story of Fern comes when one of the men who come to her confesses that he looks into her eyes as if they "held God."

Her eyes, unusually weird and open, held me. Held God. He flowed in as I've seen the countryside flow in. Seen men. I must have done something—what, I don't know, in the confusion of my emotion. She sprang up. Rushed some distance from me. Fell to her knees, and began swaying, swaying. . . . Boiling sap . . . flooded arms. . . . It found her throat, and spattered in plaintive, convulsive sounds. . . . And then she sang, brokenly, a Jewish cantor singing with a broken voice. A child's voice, or an old man's. Dusk hid her. . . . I rushed to her. She fainted in my arms.[14]

The passage instantly retreats after that climactic disclosure—as if embarrassed by its awkward daring and stream-of-consciousness "rush/spatter"—into clothing Fern afresh with the solid indifference of virgin mistress. "Nothing ever really happened. Nothing ever came to Fern, not even I. Something I would do for her. Some fine unnamed thing. . . . And, friend, you?"[15]

The rhetorical question appears to seal Fern's fate as if it is addressed in the early 1920s to a future cinema audience, whose rapture over adolescent sex-symbols discloses their own tragic roots of deprivation and starved hope that are resources to be exploited by the mass-media. What is of interest to us are curious elements of 'decadence' or intuitive transformation of rooted deprivation. Those elements are fleeting. They reflect a capacity that languishes or dies. Stone-bias of the virgin whore *moves* within a dimension of mind. The movement coincides with a fiery brushstroke or mental canvas, "boiling sap" in arms and fingers, and this is followed by broken song arching through the womb of inner landscape, inner age, inner youth, as if in lament over help-less millions destined for depression and battlefield in the 1930's and 1940s. It is as if the ground of being releases mediation be-tween partial, newborn "rush" and partial death or "faint." As a consequence, stone-bias cracks or *sings* only when it *moves* (rushes) though *still* (faint). An inner fissure appears in claustrophobic deprivation only to be blocked almost simultaneously into the epitaph of millions. How close, one wonders, is that epitaph of Fern to Gertrude of Clay's fossilised apparition of love?

All this leads us back, I think, to Titus's "little revolution in great shades."

Take, for example, "a light too violent for ghosts" into which Sourdust, Flay, Swelter and Sepulchrave vanish. These "marshaled ghosts" are deceptive. Some are "the ghost of a ghost." This is certainly the state of Swelter.[16] But Flay is an example of a *living* ghost-retainer of *dead*, apparently vanished, Sepulchrave (Titus's father). Flay was banished or sent into exile by Gertrude of Clay after Sepulchrave's death; he lives in Gormenghast Forest but still haunts the precincts of Gormenghast Castle. We shall come to Titus's encounter with Flay in the forest in a while but first let us stress the peculiar *living* opacities within *dissolving* "flay" figures akin to processes of mediation and arbitration between vanished landlord and live ghost-retainer.

Dissolution or disappearance may constitute a state or condition native to figured ghosts of the living and the dead but it may also constitute the comedy of unseen shadow cast by living ghost-retainer. That shadow is secretly bent on worming its way back into the affections of the past, it is bent on blocking its capacity for exiled creation and the birth of freedom. Thus Flay's bearing on Titus is in a context of exiled creation or hidden shadow that accumulates into a brushstroke that marks a stage in the ambiguous trespass of freedom, within Titus himself, through 'block' servants of tradition. The fugitive nature of Titus's free mind through these 'flay blocks' is assisted by apparently necessary but nightmarish concealment within the Cyclopean womb of space that Flay becomes in sheltering, yet rebuking, his young master's desire to escape from Gormenghast.

In terms of fiction, all this implies a complex strategy by gifted writers and also a capacity for altered habits of perception across generations of gifted readers in assessing paradoxes of 'legitimacy of convention' and 'illegitimacy of freedom' within a harlequin cosmos.

Take 'legitimacy' first. The "ghost of a ghost" turns into ironic legitimacy, ironic transparency, born of the clear void of ancestral death that holds Flay in thrall until his live shadow is eclipsed. The regime of legitimacy in a age such as ours seems all-powerful. It thrives, in the late twentieth century, on television convention. Television ghosts—not unlike Steerpike and other mirrored actor-characters in *Gormenghast*—remain perennial virgin retainer (Flay) or perennial virgin terrorist (Steerpike) or perennial virgin masks of destitution. Starving children remain perennial bones, the ghosts of the ghosts of tradition of famine in Africa and around the globe. Each television sketchpad, drawn by satellites, encircles the globe with the "skelton of an ostrich" through whose figurative bars audiences may enjoy surviving species, cats and birds in exotic jungles.[17] Press another rib of the ostrich and turn to legitimate dynasties, presidents and prime ministers groomed to be interviewed in suitably shadowless profile.

When Titus rebels, he begins a quest for hidden shadow in clear void. In that rebellion, the perennial ostrich undergoes the beginnings of 'illegitimate trespass' from the heights into the depths or from the depths into the dazzling shadow of the heights. The wedding of grace to animal humanity is a prime aspect of harlequin psyche; and susceptibilities to disease and to therapy of genesis are so interwoven that creation appears decadent or becomes a ceaseless, never-finished dialogue with hidden shadow.

The action of illegitimate grace cannot be proven. It lives in shadow to uproot earth in sky or sky in earth into collaborative curvature or cycles of descending stone, descending suns and stars.

Cycle of mind, or genius of love, cannot be proven. It lives in shadow imbued with symbols of long and complicated descent through mutated hierarchies of instinct that overlap spirit in the animal masks, animal fates that all religions employ—dove, lamb, tiger, lion.

'Illegitimacy' therefore is sprung from the shadow of complex freedom, a hidden shadow cast by the substance of exile. It creates interstices in, or interruptions of, the clear void's continuity of ghost genetics into the death of God and Man. It seeks to translate distinctions of invisibility, invisible life of necessity, fossilised or vanished convention that still feeds on our appetite for wealth and power.

Titus's encounter with Flay in the Forest of Gormenghast extends and deepens the paradox of live shadow we intuited in "a light too violent for ghosts." For there in the magical Forest we perceive an element that *flits* into and apparently out of the narrative strategy that Peake employs. Flay is the live retainer of the dead earl and a loyal servant to the living heir, Titus, despite his banishment into the Forest. Perhaps it is his unswerving loyalty that makes him a curiously ubiquitous spirit, a spectre of tradition that haunts the precincts of Gormenghast Castle until his spirit appears almost indistinguishable from other figured ghosts of the dead who also seem to exist everywhere and nowhere.

Titus meets Flay in the Forest—it is Titus's first attempt to fly from Gormenghast. Flay frowns upon Titus's obsession with freedom, protects the young earl, feeds him and makes certain that he returns, or is escorted back, to the Castle. During the interval that they spend together we discover that poor Flay's banishment has plucked the heart out of his breast. " 'To have your heart dug out with its long roots, Lordship—that's what exiled means,' " Flay tells Titus.[18] Flay's statement is a significant ambiguity that resembles, even as it differs from, a loss or void of conscience that Steerpike endures.

Flay's "dug-out heart" is manifestly a token of his continuing loyalty to Gormenghast in the midst of the horror of unjust banishment. As such he embodies in himself "the marshaled ghosts" of the past and trophies, skins, animal cavities, horns of slain beasts, that Gormenghast enshrines; but despite this the shadow of exiled fate (which accompanies him and pushes him into sculptures of freedom) tugs at him, pushes him beyond himself, keeps him strangely alive in spite of his flayed status of museum retainer, makes him susceptible to shapes that flit in the Forest out of the heart of animal spirit. It is as if Flay's dug-out heart begins to alchemise itself into visions that fly before him, backwards into the depths of animal space even as they seem to leap forward and to hover against a light that dazzles him with the beauty of potential freedom. This fugitive element summons him to break with the past, and leaves him torn and bewildered; he fears his visions and his alarm mounts afresh when Titus's eyes of flexible childhood light upon something Flay thought no one else saw.

"Mr. Flay," Titus whispered with a passionate urgency. "Am I dreaming?"
"No, boy."
"Then I saw it."
"Saw what Lordship? Lie quiet now—lie quiet."
"That thing in the oak woods, that flying thing."

Then, "Mr. Flay's body tautened and there was an absolute silence in the cave."[19]

There, in parenthesis, is the notion of live shadow that conceals an order of fugitive mind even as it seems to point, I would suggest, to an essential and mysterious quality of arbitration between all partial images. That quality of arbitration appears of illegitimate origin. It would seem cruel as it uproots the heart but transformative in its evolving sculptures of space, its visionary logic of freedom. Perhaps one is helped into an understanding of this by cross-cultural womb of space. Take, for example, the 'exact weight of spirit' that we pursued in Faulkner's *Intruder in the Dust*, an exactitude that led us more deeply still into paradoxes of exaggerated contour as the depths rose to meet the heights; it also led us into the intuitive mantle of the *hungan* that fell upon elderly Miss Habersham and upon the two boys Charles Mallison and Aleck Sander. *Is Flay, is the great skin or body of apparently heartless void that belongs to the Long Man of the Woods, both mantle of the* hungan *and interwoven spectre of corpse of tradition?* Is Flay a deep-seated variable of untamable myth that we encountered in aspects of Haitian *vodun* (or Voodoo) aroused into problematic decadence within neuroses of the English imagination brilliantly manifest in Peake's *Gormenghast*? It is a question that prompts us to pursue some of the admixtures of exaggerated contour of conscience and heart within *Gormenghast*.

Running parallel to Flay's great skin or Forest cave, within which Titus perceives flying illegitimate nemesis that hovers between dead institution and sculpture of freedom, is Steerpike's *conscienceless void* that comes down on the side of robot mankind (or 'sent dead') in bodies that are *technically* (but not psychically) alive. The *technical* life (*psychical* death) of Steerpike needs to be judged within associated or over-arching contours of magical cave or body within which the Child in the womb of space intuitively wrestles with the sentence of damnation Steerpike would inflict upon him.

It is important in the context of this study to address those associated contours, before we leave *Gormenghast*, for the hint they sustain of *hungan*-therapy despite robot nemesis. I shall do so first by tracing correspondences between Flay and Steerpike, then by tracing the "cocoon of compassion" that Titus inhabits fleetingly with his sister, Fuchsia, to see how this bears obliquely on Steerpike's technical motivation.

Flay's body is both his physical appearance and the environment in which he moves. Flay "shifted himself on the ledge of rock, and shrugged his high, bony shoulders up to his ears; like a vulture." Steerpike is "also high-shouldered to a degree little short of malformation. . . ."[20]

It is in the cave of sleep, as if enfolded by the gaunt, over-arching skin of Flay, that Titus glimpses through partial half-vision, half-blindness the "flying thing that floats across the trees."[21]

Steerpike is "slender and adroit of limb and frame," despite his malformation, with "eyes close-set and the colour of dried blood." Steerpike's adroitness gives him command of the roofs and walls of Gormenghast Castle, which he scales with ease. "If ever he had harboured a conscience in his tough narrow breast he has by now dug out the awkward thing. . . . The day of Titus's birth had seen the commencement of his climb across the roofs of Gormenghast

and the end of his servitude. . . ." Steerpike's acrobatics resemble
the "flying thing" that Titus had seen, except that Steerpike's
achievements are the perversity of flight. This wiry blood-
resemblance to flying sculpture of freedom in an acrobatic robot is even more marked in the fantastic ropes upon which
Steerpike swings from floor to floor, window to window, of
Gormenghast Castle. The speed with which he moves across turrets
(rather than trees into which Titus's vision disappears) earns him
his visiting card inscribed "His Infernal Slyness, the Arch-Fluke
Steerpike."[22]

Steerpike also has his wings (akin to Flay's gaunt body of a
vulture) but they are implicit in acrobatic cunning allied to
ingenious mirrors that he sets within the walls and rooms of
Gormenghast. These hidden mirrors bring to his eyes of vulturine
intensity reflected messages of the activities of all who live in the
Castle, in particular the hideous routines of Barquentine, Master of
Ritual. Steerpike's fabrication is, in effect, an architectural forest of
rooms and halls that flank a main chimney. Wires and mirrors give
him access to "occupants of de-privatized rooms" on whom his
intelligence preys.[23]

Despite differences, Steerpike's fabricated, conscienceless forest
resembles the Forest in which Flay also thrives on mirrors
born of the 'dug-out' flight of his heart within every glancing blade
or stroke of light. Flay also has his charmed collection of beasts his
intelligence surveys. His cave in the Forest serves to transport
reflected light thrown from a natural chimney formation.[24]

The body of fascinating correspondences between Flay and
Steerpike would almost seem to confirm Steerpike's ascendancy
over Flay, but an uneasy equilibrium nevertheless is maintained
between the *hungan* of freedom and the *robot* of heartless,
conscienceless void; this equilibrium is achieved, in some degree,
through the mental conversion of Flay's cave into Childhood
correspondence with a "cocoon of compassion" that Titus and his
sister, Fuchsia, momentarily inhabit.

Titus is shepherded back to Gormenghast by Flay and finds
himself facing punishment for attempting to escape. He is sustained
by Fuchsia within their cocoon or converted cave, which thrives on
darkened legacies of memory.[25]

In that "darkened legacy" one sees afresh with luminous but

indefinable exactitude the plight of Flay. Titus and Fuchsia have
been betrayed by their mother, the Countess of Groan; thus Flay's
banishment at her hands is, in a sense, theirs as well. Flay's loyalty
is pointless; he continues to serve an institution that has long cut
him adrift. Titus and Fuchsia are drawn spontaneously to seek to
convert Flay's pointless loyalty into a "cocoon of compassion."
This does not, however, lessen the pointlessness of Flay's
affections, which block radical innovation and conspire
unwittingly with subversion and terrorism masked by Steerpike's
"Infernal Slyness."

It is Titus's and Fuchsia's mental conversion of Flay's cave that
reflects, I find, upon Flay's capacity to draw into himself them and
other creatures, childhood fantasy as well as charmed beasts, all of
whom he stores in his mirrors and whose magical tone differs from
Steerpike's deadly storage of "de-privatized rooms." Steerpike lives
because of others' pointless affection for, and pointless loyalty to,
institutions that have ceased to evolve and are sustained not only
by flayed retainers but by fantasy-youth and symbolic childhood
of Titus and Fuchsia.

On one occasion, Steerpike scales his spidery ropes and ladders
to visit Fuchsia but freezes into immobility despite his amazing
skills and is unable to descend from windowsill to floor of the
room. Fuchsia now has him captive, as if he were a lifeless, cosmic
doll, but with a pointless gesture from her "he suddenly came to life
again, as though a trigger had been touched" in him by her.[26] Their
doll-like affair seems fated to destroy worlds.

Fuchsia wears a crimson dress that gives her the appearance of a
painting that is poised to move, yet seems only cinematically active
and devoid of creative movement through Nature, or devoid of
capacity for translated being or inner re-dress of fixed boundaries.
As a consequence she remains "starved for sunbeams."[27] Such
starvation parodies the live shadow explored in this chapter,
though something coheres of "infinite subtlety" that resembles
Flay's enigmatic existence within "marshaled ghosts" overtaken by
a "violent light," and brings poignancy and tragedy to her half-
mutual doll/half-mutual flesh-and-blood affair with Steerpike in
the gesture that brings him back to life. All these interwoven
distinctions make *Gormenghast* not only a major but a unique
English novel saturated with memorable, fantastic and darkened

legacies. The difficulty it raises in regard to the creation of movement across fixed boundaries of institution implies a complex deprivation that cries out soundlessly, as in a dream.

The gestation of capacity for transformed age remains incestuously bewildered in *Gormenghast* and, though in individual tone and style it differs from Ellison's Trueblood intercourse with Matty Lou, I find parallels between surreal Trueblood's "flying geese" and the precocious Gormenghast brother and sister, the ghost-father and dug-out heart of banished retainer, which reflects freedom and authority in disarray.

Flay's charmed beasts in the Forest and Steerpike's "de-privatized" inmates of Gormenghast come to reflect a tragic impasse, against which Titus's "little revolution" pits itself.

Thought and Action

The gulf between thought and action is clearly a complicated humour of childhood, adolescence and so-called maturity, the games civilisation plays on itself through inherent associations and exaggerated contours of heart and conscience. Of even more ancient lineage is the habit the thinking mind wears to avoid acting in compliance with thought or creative conscience and against apparent self-interest or economic privilege. Literature has its problematic and threatened place in a competitive world of realistic self-interest(s), and poetries and fictions compete not only with tangible goods and commodities but with intangibles that plague the mind within "the meaninglessness and futility" of life, in Eliot's phrase. The construction of elaborate weaponries and armies is realistically necessary in a world of great superpowers. . . . Deprivation becomes as endemic as inflation, armaments as endemic as world poverty. For example, the Soviet Union's invasion of Afghanistan in 1979 was launched, the Russians said, to preserve stability, and this—they claimed—was their 'realist' goal. The Afghans and the Third World saw it differently. What is apparently realist policy in one military light is realist fallacy or humiliation in another stranglehold of circumstance.

As a consequence, the humour of parody infects individual imaginations. Cross-cultural 'jokes', 'black comedy' parables seek to re-dress polarised thought and action across frontiers and boundaries. Emma Tennant's *The Last of the Country House Murders* may be read, I find, as a bizarre entertainment and a serious comedy rooted in the endemic deprivations of a realistic age.[28]

Ostensibly the novel is set in an England which has been over-taken by an abortive socialist revolution that has largely destroyed both the fabric and the potential for original imagination and original action; but the true setting is 'everywhere and nowhere' within an artificial, global landscape haunted by mental images of dragon's teeth that mimic epical action, in the wake of futile and barren thought.

There are disguised allusions to the Golden Fleece and Jason and Medea, to which I shall return in a little while. There are allusions to a host of writers in whom action and thought possess degrees of sophisticated alienation—Henry James, Henrik Ibsen, Samuel Beckett, Dorothy Sayers, Noel Coward and others; the choice is so varied that it is calculated, I think, to set in train an intuitive, perhaps unprovable, jigsaw which may evoke other unstated or famous talents. One thinks of Gogol's *Dead Souls* or Rulfo's *Pedro Páramo*.

All cultures reflect a psychical jigsaw in the stars, whether in astrological investitures that clothe the dead or in astronomical snapshots of the cradle of the universe, and the alienated spectre of thought and action may well occur when the birth of fact is so rigidly pigmented that it ceases to be true. It becomes a statistic of dead souls qualified to vote in rigged elections, or a series of faded postcards and family heirlooms qualified to live the lives of a vanished middle/upper-middle class.

In our age of extraordinary astronomical discovery, one would assume that unprecedented enlightenment has been born, that a marriage with asymmetric riddles is within our grasp, but this would be a complacent assumption. Astronomers need no longer the excommunication of the Church to win enduring fame. Their excommunication is accomplished by the rule of dogmatic common sense over the incalculables of truth, and also by a divorce between art and science. Thus, enduring fame in the realm of common sense and divorce of art from science tends to become a parody of imaginative genius and to invite notions that Man is a genetic robot within a mock-inventive, mock-political, mock-epical universe. Cedric Brown is the 'Master of the Joke' (rather than the Master of Ritual in Gormenghast age) in Emma Tennant's bleak comedy.

His excommunication of astronomy is a major tongue-in-cheek or eye-in-skull performance.

Cedric had seen that there was no universe at all. There was the sun; and earth, of course, with its billions of inhabitants . . . and there was the moon, as the astronauts had proved. And there was nothing else! The stars were optical illusions . . . a fault in man's make-up. . . . The pin-pricks of light in the eyes of a cat were more tangible than Mars or Saturn, the Milky Way a corneal smudge. . . .[29]

Cedric's "corneal smudge" and triumph of dogmatic common sense is the strength of his 'dug-out' eye and intuitive kinship with Gormenghast's Steerpike and Flay. Cedric is also to play at being a prime suspect in "the last country house murder" to be staged in his mock-socialist Utopia engineered by political scientists or robots and mock-geniuses. The murder is planned by the government itself as a considerable tourist attraction in the heartland of England within a stone's throw of Stonehenge.

Cedric is a world-famous professional actor with a practical interest in "the necropolis of beehive-shaped houses" that constitute his international audience of the dead under a "starless sky" in which he is nevertheless a superstar.[30]

No one seeing Cedric Brown for the first time would have considered him a potential menace to society. Like most actors he had a kind of non-face, a rubbery stretch of skin like an old canvas that has been painted over by several artists in succession and still shows traces of the landscape or portrait beneath.[31]

Cedric "climbs into his white helicopter and sets the automatic pilot to West Wiltshire . . . to murder an old friend for the sake of the tourist trade.[32] That old friend is Jules, as we shall see, whose ex-fiancee Bessie still wishes to "marry and/or kill" him for reasons that go back a long way into obscure places and journeys that they have made together. Cedric has been cast—as already indicated—to kill Jules as a tourist trade stunt that will capture the eyes of the world. So, if he is to kill for the sake of the tourist trade, it will also be for the sake of chameleon movies which haunt every run-down as well as emblazoned cinema around the globe. On arrival at the country house where the crime is to be performed he is recognised by crowds as a twentieth century great. Are these crowds real or are they snapshot multitudes on a gigantic screen? Are they a gigantic hoax?

"It's Bogie!"
Hands reach up to him, smiles break out on sullen faces. *From the long years of apathy and deprivation, the only diversion old movies and intolerable soap operas, the hero had come at last to the rescue* [italics mine].[33]

Cedric is greeted by a babble of voices, South London accents, West Indian accents, Liverpool accents. Women scream as he depresses his lip and smiles like a gangster. Then, with another twitch of the facial muscles, he assumes the mask of a Fagin, a hunted creature. The fascination of the crowd rises to a new crescendo of welcome when his posture and expression change again. The crowd suddenly turns rigid. It seems to stretch for miles like a great army that has sprung from the ground. That army cries "Mein Fuehrer."

Cedric's movie has invoked the mythical dragon's teeth that spring to attention in the shape of a great army out of the ground. He is both actor and practical joker; his shadow on the screen invokes millions—the sown teeth of the camera—and he becomes Jason-Fuehrer. The aspect of "fuehrer" is soon submerged as unpalatable practical joke, but that of ambiguous Jason remains to incorporate Jules into itself. The stage is now set for Jason (or Jules) to be shot by his enraged ex-fiancée or bride or bride-to-be Bessie or Medea. Bessie thinks of Jules, "who had ruined the fine, smooth path of her life. Whom she would now marry or kill. It occurred to Bessie, thickened though her features had become with nostalgic tears, her eyes crooked with the effort of summoning them, that it was time she made up her mind. . . . As Medea she towered in the bed-chamber, sending icy vibrations. . . ."[34]

The practical joke that Cedric plays on himself, in donning the *persona* of Jules, possesses the flicker of untamable myth, for though it was second or third or fourth 'tamed' nature, so to speak, for him to assume the mask of a Bogie, of Fagin, of Jason-Fuehrer, of Jason-Jules, the penultimate and last characterisations were *out of step* with the role he had been asked to play by the State. It was as if he saw his tamed reflection in the mirror or screen of planned events assume a rebellious life of its own. There had been suggestions in Emma Tennant's half-surreal narrative that this was subtly happening to all of the characters, that their reflected or screened images could rebel into unpredictable dimensions as in a mirror, where feet that advance could suddenly rebel and achieve a retreating reflection, hands that fall could suddenly raise themselves, bodies that sat before the mirror could rebel by standing in the mirror. . . . And the rebellious, subtle sum-total of this comes to a climax in Cedric's practical joke. He is *married to* and *killed by* Medea/Bessie within the very Jules/Jason mask or image of a friend that he is himself cast by the State to kill. He is overtaken or triggered into 'out-of-step' perspective by Jules through whom he suffers at Bessie/Medea's hands the death he intended to inflict.

With Cedric's marriage to Bessie, the practical joke begins to expire, but the flicker of a deeper untamable comedy emerges in "the last of the country house murders." An inverse parallel, it seems, relates Cedric's and Bessie's marriage-in-death to the pointless trigger through which Gormenghast's Fuchsia brings Steerpike back to life. The nemesis of pointless order, pointless regime, is intuitively re-dressed or converted into a daemonic cross-cultural paradox. Steerpike lives. Jason perishes.

Is Fuchsia herself a doll-like Medea? Is Steerpike a deranged robot of the Golden Fleece? Are his diabolic mirrors also susceptible to reflections that rebel, as if to portray alienations of ritual action and rebellious psyche or thought?

Zero re-dress involves us, I think, in a conversion of the practical joke of 'non-existence' (or 'blanket function') into comedy which builds 'character' out of the sediment of history. This principle is not foreign to folk interpretations of dreams: the dream of *faeces* for example means *money* in folk wisdom; the dream conspires with nature to play a 'joke' on a society where god is mammon. Illegitimate blanket, so to speak—the marriage of faeces and money—precipitates the child of god who 'unseals' character in the shock of laughter's community, purgation of the highest in the lowest, the shock of stretched and evolving awareness.

Thus it is arguable that 'character' may arise through fissures in 'block' function (masked as god) that metamorphoses into a treasure/comedy of an unpredictable range of sensibility pitched into and arising from abysses of the heights and the depths. Precarious originality—tested and re-tested breaches of 'block function' into illuminating riddles of sensibility—is the evolution of character, and in that context character emerges almost unconsciously out of the cross-cultures of active reflections cast upon the canvas of time in surprised and surprising ways.

Such fissure or shock of surprise is, I find, at the heart of Claude Simon's *The Flanders Road*, which appeared in France in 1960 and was translated into English by Richard Howard in 1962.[35] The true substance of character in that unusual novel becomes both precarious and measureless, not wholly soil or seed from which it arises, trunk or branch or leaf, animal or vegetable, star or shell, in which it clothes its fears or hopes in a landscape of war. The traffic of armies across the landscape of a civilisation, divided and segmented in itself, is also a blanket of unawareness—a walking sleep—between functional animal and functional animal, between apparently robot horse and apparently robot rider, between deadening pain and conscript duty, between suicide and glory, between authoritarian and permissive dreams of death and love.

Within and against such densities of unawareness, it is the *shock* of paradoxical disclosure that creates the lightning mutuality of universal character; though darkness falls again, it falls with a different tone to heighten or deepen the convertibility of blanket materials, functions, deprivations. Tone and convertibility coincide, therefore, with abrupt disclosure and penetration of walking blanket in isolated, however efficient function, which divides regiment from regiment, conscript being from conscript being, faeces-man from foetal-man. The image of blanket takes one's mind back, I think, to Gormenghast's "dug-out" heart in the Forest of magical skins inhabited by functional Flay, which yields nevertheless the "cocoon of compassion" that Titus and Fuchsia half-blindingly, yet with lightning intuition, come to inhabit for a moment or two.

The Flanders Road throws its own functional skin or flayed reality over Captain de Reixach's bullet-ridden, 'dug-out' heart, and our first intimation of shocked dream or living sculpture of resurrected being in Claude Simon's art comes within "an army on the march surprised by a cataclysm."[36] Reixach lives again through three dragoons who served with him in the campaign of Belgium in 1940. They have suffered a measure of that "cataclysm." The carapace of object-function that enfolds them has partly flashed open like a door in a storm. Their conversations and reminiscences achieve 'disjointed' coherence. Reixach returns through them, through their darkened legacies of memory, as if in part from within half-lightning, half-shrouded sediment of place. He arises also from the practical mud or humour of cast-away resources of humanity that they invoke.

The distance between individuals, walking skins wrapped up in their own occasion or performance, can appear unbridgeable.

The progress of time itself, that is, invisible immaterial neither beginning nor end nor point of reference at the heart of which he had the sensation of remaining frozen, stiff on his horse that was also invisible in the darkness among the phantoms of cavalrymen . . . the whole regiment seemed to advance without progression, like those pantomimists whose legs imitate the movement of walking while behind them a trembling canvas backdrop unrolls on which are painted houses trees clouds, with this difference that here the canvas backdrop was only night, blackness. . . .[37]

The 'invisibility of time' augments the functional blanket between object-persons, invisible to each other within their seal of instrumentality. The emphasis on regimented person as insensible object is woven into "painted houses trees clouds" within "a trembling canvas." That 'tremor' partially contradicts "a [functional] advance without progression."

"An army on the march [is] surprised by a cataclysm." Lightning awareness is the genesis of seeing through 'invisibles' or 'brute functions' into the curious mind of active reflection. That mind *astonishes* even when it seems to confirm what one thinks one has seen before; above all it confounds, confuses ultimately, the reinforcement of biased habit or authoritarian eclipse within the blanket of war.

The term *cataclysm* is itself a deceptive notion. One may illustrate the implications in the following way. An aeroplane that functions admirably and insensibly within terrifying turbulences high in the sky may crash if softly throttled by a flock of birds when it takes off from the ground. As a functional object its blind strength succumbs to the gravity of a pillow of feathers in the walking sleep of technology. Such 'passive' gravity, such pillow, may well prove a 'cataclysm', whereas the turbulent storm does not. The apparently invincible and frozen psychological climate that tends to arm an object or person—to give it its apparatus of indifference in pursuit of its operations—suffers a minute flash of lightning perception akin to a dreamer's flock of feathers. This may appear cataclysmic in terms of the train of disaster that follows, but in essence it is a thread of revelation, it is fissured block however saturated at later stages with remorse, with helplessness or sorrow, in the predicament of isolated function it discloses.

The flash of insight speaks of the complexity of mental spirit and dialogue between diverse creations, inventions, creatures. It subsists on the shadow of terrifying hope or therapeutic community beyond every indifferent universe. But it may come so late, or be apprehended so late, within the medium of robot performance, that its flash or 'fissure' fails to open a path between 'function' and 'function', and a train of wreckage in the wake of so-called cataclysm follows.

These are considerations that seem to me to reside tentatively and dialectically in the very 'painted' bleakness of *The Flanders Road*, where 'cataclysm' is as much a 'splinter' as a 'glacier'. Cataclysm is "a slow advancing glacier . . . a faint tinkle of glass. . . ."[38]

That "glass" matches the grain of vulnerability in an objective person, it shadows or paints a thread of movement in the invisible mind, invisible time, of place upon the dying Captain de Reixach "as if he and his horse had been cast together out of one and the same material, a grey metal, the sun glinting for a second on the naked blade then everything man horse and sabre—collapsing together sideways like a lead soldier . . . behind the carcass of that burnt truck abandoned there . . . in the brilliant spring afternoon. . . ."[39]

The implications of 'still' movement within collapsing order, a 'movement' that intuitively re-dresses boundaries of tone and feeling, have been visualised in different ways in previous chapters. We looked at the implications of 'still', 'moving' landscape (reflected in the virgin whore Fern). Jean Toomer, the black

American writer, wrote *Cane* in the early 1920s some forty years or so before the appearance of *The Flanders Road*. The asymmetric involvement of 'movement' in 'invisible time' in *The Flanders Road* occupies *Gormenghast* as well, though there are elusive distinctions in the 'mind-of-place' Fern who *sings*, the painted Fuchsia who *bleeds* a deprivation of 'mind-of-the-sun', the 'flesh' of glass in *The Flanders Road* that is the shadow of lightning-mind, human revelation or astonished mirror of war.

It is the cross-cultural apparition within partial manifestations of evolving character—in 'sculptured' song, in 'sacrificed, harlequin' sun, in fragile yet immortal *coniunctio* of mind and cosmos—that alerts us to the arbitration of shared genius within ethnic bodies, black and white, that are invisible to each other within a blanket of functional, if not racially biased, scholarship.

The *Cyclopean eye* is an imprint of fear (see Chapter Three) and it acquires new peculiar anthropological undertones in *The Flanders Road*. In the legends of Reixach's family are ambiguous ancestors, half-horse, half-men, as though the myth of the centaur secretes an anthropological corridor of escape from the giant of war that cannibalises cultures. Odysseus escaped the Cyclops by riding under the belly of a ram, half-man, half-ram. So too half-human centaur seeks to deceive the hands of the giant of war with contours of flesh whose grain or sculpture is more animal than human. But the deception is thwarted or tainted, as one cannot but perceive in the following mosaic of reflection and conversation between Reixach's dragoons.

> 'I'd just like to see him once without his boots on. . . . Just to make sure he doesn't have hoofs instead of feet . . .'
>
> Georges thinking . . . of all those enigmatic dead men, frozen and solemn in their gilded frames, . . . and among which featured prominently that portrait . . . (that distant progenitor, sire) which had *in his forehead a red hole* from which the blood ran down . . . standing there, impassive, equine and decorous at the heart of a permanent aura of mystery and violent death [italics mine].[40]

The birth of the Reixach Odyssey legend—in which Georges, the dragoon, shares himself as a distant relation to the Reixach family—possesses a central ambiguity. The half-animal saviour upon which half-human ancestor rides out of the blood-stained cave of cannibal Cyclops is adorned with the mask of the Cyclops itself, "in his forehead a red hole." The riddle of ancestral, protective beast proves itself in the mutual and stricken flesh of half-giant, half-victim, that appears to the dragoons in the Belgian campaign as forerunner of the death of their captain. It comes at the end of a long and gruelling march when "they looked at the horse still lying on its side at the back of the stables: . . . *Only the eye still looked alive . . . gentle cyclopean stare, accusing and moist*" [italics mine].[41]

The Cyclopean self-accusation raises the enigma of ancestral parenthesis and glory in the hunt of war, and of the birth of fame masked by self-destructive motivation, *by a desire for suicide*, which has been gestating in the womb of cannibal civilisation for generations. Priceless animal species around the globe are being destroyed and remain in danger of extinction, and horse and man become a measure of bewildered half-giant, half-victim, which leads us back to thwarted *coniunctio* and to the fragility of ancestral dominations within incestuous, ecstatic 'trueblood'.

One of Reixach's dragoons was a former jockey in the Reixach stable in civilian life. That jockey became Reixach's wife's lover. He takes her in the stable where she is in terror of being found out. Their love affairs have an urgent, sensuous pace. In the half-dark stables her white thighs flash, "her eyes wild, her neck twisted."[42]

The wild eyes, the twisted neck, are another equine shadow, no longer impassive and decorous as perceived in the portrait of ancient progenitor and sire but still emblematic of an equation between the mystery of love and "violent death." And this raises the last issue I would like to explore in *The Flanders Road* concerning Captain de Reixach's deliberate exposure of himself to enemy bullets or steel; namely, "that suicide which the war gave him."[43]

We may approach this mask of military glory worn by Reixach by returning to the notion of 'cataclysm' discussed in this chapter. 'Cataclysm' has many concentric horizons in *The Flanders Road*. Its invisible epicentre creates shock waves around which ancestral jealousies, monotonies, stubbornness, circle like "insects suspended in the twilight" of an age.[44]

On one of these waves or horizons, Captain de Reixach marries his virgin whore, twenty years younger than he. On another, his wife's 'stable-affair' with the jockey parodies the image of ancestral master saddled by and saddling his slain mount. A momentum is established which distributes the weight and paralysis of riding function, crest or wave; it is akin to the nemesis of tradition in its revelation of illegitimate ancestry, uncertain bloodlines through virgin but promiscuous brides over the centuries that haunt Reixach's twentieth-century marriage. It confirms the mixed or centaur badge that Reixach wears but leaves him so desolate that he comes by degrees into a state of mind which *rejects* the ambiguity of ancestry. The sole alternative by which he seeks to restore a virginal brilliance to tainted half-giant, half-victim, lies in the purity of steel, sabre or bullet, on the field of battle. As he collapses on that field "the sun's dazzling reflection condensed . . . glory on *that virginal steel* . . . [italics mine]." Reixach may well have recalled his wife at that instant, as the dragoons imply. He knew of her promiscuity when he married her and this knowledge was the beginning of his consumption of "that Passion" that marked the brow of his distant progenitor and sire.

Captain de Reixach's suppressed or hypothetical need of a virgin tradition, his ambiguous marriage and relationships, constellates the Passion of the Centaur, the "red hole" in the forehead of ancient progenitor that becomes the imprint of *virgin* steel, sabre or bullet, on one hand, even as it pools on the other hand the stigmata of decadence upon feared animal antecedents, loathed animal heart, head, womb.

The compulsion to suicide may, therefore, be read even more deeply as the repudiation of 'illegitimate horseplay' written into enigmatic bloodlines; these become the practical joke of the gods, recalling the joke or birth of Helen from the egg of a swan woven into the epicentre of the Trojan War. This is what Reixach can no longer stomach in the sniggering, debased, epic shell of rumour that clothes his wife's promiscuity in the chatter of stable boys and bedroom maids. At the same time, he has no intention of surrendering the apparatus of the centaur which—with its animal saviour within Cyclopean cave or womb of the hunt—is a necessary ritual mask to be penetrated, generation after generation, by virgin bullet or steel in the heart as well as brow. On that wave or saddled horizon Reixach consumed the harlequin mystery of love and "violent death."

This is the inverse of the vision explored earlier in this study, in which I suggested that the alchemy of evolution bears lightning perceptions that are potential therapy within the blanket of isolated function or 'object' condition that conscripts the human person. The essential difference in my conceptions and Claude Simon's lies in subsistence on illegitimate descent, so to speak, from both the heights and the depths, so that art may possess an equation with evolution as well as grace, with animal mutations as well as dark comedy and terrifying (because mystically shrouded) compassion of god. In *The Flanders Road*, however, the Eliotesque horror of impure evolution prevails. It is instinctive to Cyclopean guilt and centaur sexuality. The virgin structure of legitimate order reifies itself therefore—if it exists at all—in the bliss of hidden compulsions toward suicide within dignified, professional activities, such as war or any other vocation that may mask the act of suicide.

The Flanders Road is a consummate and brilliant example of the mystery of the virgin whore as a catalyst not of heterogeneous elements in creative counterpoint, but of unacknowledged, unfashionable and therefore suppressed guilt that can only be borne in ritual games of the extinction of species, animal and human, man and god, wherein the central clown or despairing warrior/huntsman weds the slain beast and receives its mortal wound administered by dazzling reflection on virginal bullet or steel.

Our last novel in this cross-cultural exploration is *Nightwood* by the American writer Djuna Barnes.[46] Barnes's complexly written, intensely moving work appeared in the mid-1930s, indeed not long before the Belgian campaign that is the setting of *The Flanders Road*, published twenty-five years or so after *Nightwood*. I mention this because with hindsight the implications that reside in *Nightwood*—whose setting ranges across the late nineteenth century into the first quarter of the twentieth century in Europe and America—seem curiously prophetic of the alienated mind that is one of the characteristics of the Second World War. High among alienated rituals of thought and action, is the programme of genocide inflicted on the Jews by Nazi Germany. In what degree, one cannot but wonder, were the Nazis driven by suicidal but controlled lusts that they projected on others rather than on themselves—by a desire to kill humanity in order to maintain the escutcheon of pure race?

One may only raise such questions, because within the hubris of sovereign strait-jacket that has long dominated imperial civilisations, we lack a profound, cross-cultural anthropology of imaginative arts, myth, culture, science, through which to break the insensibility of 'object-function' that regiments (or divides) intelligence and creativity until a distinction between the two is virtually lacking. This means the bizarre possibility exists that the responses of an 'intelligent' robot, "uninhabited" by spirit or imagination, may come to be regarded as superior to the vulnerable genius of a painter such as Van Gogh or a jazz musician such as Duke Ellington, except that the involuntary consequences may be so unpredictable that the robot 'intelligence' may come to appreciate how mechanically enclosed it is and acquire therefore the stigmata of being a human void or "uninhabited angel."

The tragedy is visible in the "uninhabited angels" of *Nightwood* draped by compulsive fabrications of heavens and damnations. The harlequin, apparently doomed, Dr Matthew-Mighty-Dante-O'Connor tells the equally harlequin, apparently doomed, Norah Flood on their last meeting in *Nightwood*, "The blessed face! It should be seen only in profile, otherwise it is observed to be the conjunction of the identical cleaved halves of sexless misgiving! Their kingdom is without precedent. . . . The uninhabited angel!" Norah Flood asks, "Perhaps, Matthew, there are devils? . . . Perhaps they have set foot in the uninhabited. Was I her devil trying to bring her comfort?"[47]

The linking of "blessed face" and "devil" casts its strangely archaic shadow over heavens and hells that continue to pursue the uninhabited angels of *Nightwood*. In the particular context of the dialogue between Matthew-Dante-O'Connor and Norah Flood, Norah was referring to Robin Vote to whom, in her own words, she tried "to bring comfort" like a devil that "sets foot in the uninhabited." Robin Vote is the prime "uninhabited angel" in whom it is possible to discern the stigmata of many cultures that run in parallel perceptions of inner void.

"So love, when it has gone, taking time with it, leaves a memory of its weight."[48] That "memory" is void of spirit that apes or is aped by "sexless misgiving" in which men and women become the debris of cataclysm. Thus Dr Matthew-Dante-O'Connor heals by misgiving or self-condemned vocation, for he too has foundered. He is driven to employ his talents upon a borderline of desperate response to inner and outer casualty within which all the *Nightwood* characters appear to suffer, Gentile, Jew, Hindu, white, black, and so on, as they seek pointlessly to embrace each other.

Matthew-Dante-O'Connor's desolation is his addiction to unending fabrications, unending fictions, which he cannot decipher as imaginative truth or sophisticated lie, and this soulless misgiving, however attractive to his many patients, friends and followers, seems to dog him not only in Norah Flood's and Robin Vote's age but apparently far back in "pre-historic memory" of the fall of Man, when he settled into the debris like chameleon-foetus of space to be flocked by "people coming to me to learn of degradation and the night."[49]

In each age, Dante-O'Connor's hell is populated by Robin Votes and Norah Floods and Jenny Petherbridges amongst others, and circus clowns of all persuasions—cloven man from woman, woman from man. His void of spirit claims to heal their "sexless misgiving," and this hypothecation almost seems, when one reads the implications closely, to run in inverse and perverse parallel with lightning perception of therapeutic genesis outlined earlier in this chapter, lightning pathway through 'block functions' in which it may be possible to interpret debris or fall in another light.

Matthew-Dante is driven, for example, to hunt through repetitive fabrications and unicorn masquerades for Robin Vote's 'flayed body' or hide, which deceives all cultures with the lie of pigmentation, 'pure' white or 'pure' black.

In attempting to console the falsely titled Jew, Baron Felix Volkbein, whom Robin married or possessed and then as unpredictably and devilishly deserted after bearing him a "mentally deficient child," Matthew-Dante equates Robin with a creature whose "hide was a river of sorrow. . . . Her eyelashes were gray-black, like the eyelashes of a nigger, and at her buttocks' soft centre a pulse throbbed like a fiddle. . . . Yes, oh God, Robin was beautiful.'. . . Sort of fluid blue under her skin, as if the hide of time had been stripped from her and with it, all transactions with knowledge. . . . A face that will age only under the blows of perpetual childhood. The temples like those of young beasts cutting horns. . . ."[50]

Who and what is Robin? Does she wear "fluid blue under her skin" as if to mourn a black unicorn, that rarest of souls that she may have once been in trampling auction block worlds? The ambiguities that stalk Poe's world become a mystical obsession in Djuna Barnes's *Nightwood*, as if to underpin Norah Flood's compulsive need of Robin Vote at the "liar's door" which opens unexpectedly not so much to let her enter, in the mask of a devil, but upon "purity's black backside" that Norah may have once bought or sold in antecedent or "prehistoric memory."[51]

Thus "purity's black [or white] backside" becomes the confessional of an auction block age, the cornerstone of an edifice of merchandised bodies apparently free to traffic with fabrications but never more exploited or unfree.

T. S. Eliot's prefatory note on *Nightwood*, which he wrote in 1937, refers to a "quality of horror and doom very nearly related to that of Elizabethan tragedy." The shadow of coming events was to justify that judgement. Even so, a work of the imagination is not so much prophetic as an intuitive capacity to secrete parallels into infinity, backward and forward, outward and inward, as it were, in the womb of space. One such parallel, it seems to me, bears on the decades of 1970s and 1980s. *Nightwood*, needless to say, is not a clinically realistic fiction, yet a comparison with clinically realistic drama, nude theatre, and the like of the 1970s and 1980s, may prove illuminating.

Contemporary cinema, television and theatre are haunted by clinical and commercial sensationalism. Killings or rape or acts of intercourse are portrayed as luridly and as exactly as possible with naked commerce of detail. The time may almost be upon us when the knife that kills will be pursued every inch of the way by x-ray camera to inform us where or when it touches a vital organ within the envelope of flesh it slits and sells to the public as entertainment. Such a clinical camera 'knows', one would think, that bodies act to mimic sexual intercourse, that the slain or raped woman or man is inevitably an actor or actress after all who arises behind the scenes when the curtain falls. But even were verisimilitude pursued to its logical conclusion, bodies were depicted in active intercourse, killed characters were actually knifed or shot (actors' bodies would then become astronomically dear), would not the *Nightwood* "liar's door" or 'curtain' that falls still be the climax of an illusion built into vicarious public consumption of riddles of love and death?

Nightwood answers this question with its obsessional gravity and curious wrath, which would resist cinematic manipulation were an attempt made to film the novel. The shadow of time in the fiction—its *visualisations* of sculpture, its plastic rhythm—is inimitably a verbal image in an almost suffocatingly real "liar's" feast, robot "liar's" spirit, fabrication of statistics or "liar's" scholarship.

The links, then, between *Nightwood* of the 1930s and late twentieth-century hollow verisimilitude are both startling and subtle. They are startling in that the long shadow of reflective action across the landscape of an age can only be sustained and genuinely cast by riddles of myth and passion sprung from the depths and the heights. Such riddles make for unconscious equation between 'hollow body' in realist theatre and "uninhabited angel" in *Nightwood*; they equate also *Nightwood's* inverse characters with x-ray potential drama of murder and sex. Such equations are rooted in a shadow that is real—terrifyingly so, perhaps, in relation to the distances that exist between "uninhabited angel" and invisible mind of cosmos. Such distances cannot but signify in themselves a riddle of epicentre, in which 'clinical' bodies possessing the thrust of metaphor associated with medical theatre run in perverse, hideous parallel with lightning perceptions of therapeutic genesis.

SEVEN
Artifice and Root

Consume my heart away
W. B. Yeats
(Sailing to Byzantium)

The nineteenth century was an age of unparallelled emigration in modern times as Irish, Poles, Scots, Welsh, English, Spanish, Portuguese, French, Italians, Germans, amongst many others, sailed across the Atlantic from Europe into the Americas. One may visualise this movement as coming in the wake of forced African labour by way of the Middle Passage; in concert with nineteenth-century Irish, Poles and others, came indentured servants, as they were called, from India and China to work upon the sugar plantations of the West Indies and British Guiana after the emancipation and flight of the African slaves from their 'theatres of cruelty'.

There are no records of a nineteenth-century Artaud or a nineteenth-century Soyinka of the Caribbean, yet the 1830s were the beginning of a 'road' into the ramshackle, urban centres of the new world of the Caribbean and into further and novel 'theatres of cruelty'. A new problematic trail also began to penetrate largely unknown interiors and other landscapes of the Americas.

No study, as far as I am aware, has been made of the arts of transplanted peoples in order to assess a kind of seismic quality in a changing culture, an epicentre that releases a suddenly fissured crack, a suddenly penetrated wall or door, through 'object' or 'slave' functions consolidated in plantation psychologies. All this bears, as it were, on the 'blood of artifice', artificial cities and so on into which new and painful roots descend. I speak of 'artifice' in the Yeatsian sense to imply *unravelled* diseased times that begin an alteration in a body of conditioned habit or response to fate, economic and cultural fate.

Such a study of Caribbean and Guianese society in the nineteenth century may have proved invaluable in coming to grips with an innovative Caribbean literary tradition in the twentieth century. My intention in this closing chapter on 'the womb of space' is to examine one aspect, nothing more, of 'artifice and root' in the twentieth century, which has been an age of unparalleled movement and an age of profound exile.

My focus is on Caribbean poetry, but it is impossible not to be conscious of Europe, Asia, Africa and the Americas, and of other poetries that bear profoundly on interwoven tapestries of movement around the globe. So we shall also touch upon a few African poets and a Pakistani-born poet, and draw upon cross-cultural implications with Europe.

The state of exile that is native, I believe, to the Caribbean poet is disputed by public relations establishments which plump for poets who 'live at home', as the saying goes. Such exercises, however, are as facile as tourist brochures and they endorse the predicament of the imaginative arts within the West Indies. Emma Tennant's "last country [or plantation?] house murder" for the sake of the tourist industry is more apt than one would think. It is hard for anyone—however entrenched are public hypocrisies—to deceive oneself that the Caribbean poet is not at odds with the philistine establishment of the West Indies. Even so, I was astonished to learn from a poet of international reputation that the establishment tends to kill the promotion of imaginative writers and critics who are members of the faculties of institutions of learning. It would seem that the very publication of controversial work by poets who are members of faculty is a red rag to the establishment bull.

The poet's economic status in the West Indies is nil unless he happens to have a doggerel political voice; poets receive reluctant fees, if any, from publishers of anthologies, magazines or newspapers. A poet's state of 'exile' in his or her own country is endemic; inevitably poets have turned to Europe or the United States, where they have emigrated across generations that include Jamaican Claude McKay, French Guianese Leon Damas, Martiniquan Aimé Césaire, amongst others. Derek Walcott was born in Saint Lucia, has apparently settled in Trinidad, but lives and works in the United States. Edward Kamau Brathwaite was born in Barbados, has his home apparently in Jamaica, but travels a great deal and has lived and worked for long periods in Africa and Europe. These paradoxes—the paradoxes of 'artifice'—are such that the Caribbean poet's authentic intuitions have begun to disclose major possibilities in making poetry respond to the problematic origins of twentieth-century community.

What do we mean by 'blood' of artifice or roots of 'artifice'? In what degree is the old plantation drumbeat capable of conversion into 'artifice' of *sound and depth* through which to visualise 'native' contours close to heart's blood in an apparently alien land? In what degree is imagistic light and dark close to unravelled *paint* (verbal, metaphoric paint) through which are created sensations of the mystery of place, inner sun, seeing night? In what degree is imagistic word close to unravelled, metaphoric sculptures through which we intuit the genesis of memory within block slave, block commander (in the Poesque sense) in expedition across worlds old and new?

It is illuminating, for instance, to approach the 'blood' of 'artifice' in Aimé Césaire's long epic poem *Return to My Native Land* and to sense parallel extremities in W. B. Yeats's *Sailing to Byzantium*. These parallel extremities involve the 'consumption' of ritual and insensible organs into re-awakened body-poetic of the imagination, body-poetic of expedition into a new world or an old world that is ceasing to be what it seemed before.

> At the end of the small hours the sun that
> coughs and spits its lungs out
>
>   . . .
>
> my beggary's living zero.[1]

Césaire's poem differs radically in tone from Yeats's:

Consume my heart away . . .
                                       and gather me
Into the artifice of eternity.[2]

Yet in essence the thrust of the poems is startlingly and
provocatively parallel in the vein of metamorphosis or "artifice of
eternity." The 'consumption' of ritual organ, heart or lung, is the
art of the Yeatsian "dying animal" through which to throw a bridge
across worlds and to make native and miraculously alive what is
alien or apparently doomed. Yeats's Byzantium is closer to Greece
than is Césaire's dream of a "native land," but a subtle equation
exists between Yeats's "hammered gold" born of consumed heart
and Césaire's "sun." *Sailing to Byzantium* images the 'blood' of
gold as the poet "consumes [his] heart away." *Return to My Native
Land* equates zero re-dress, "beggary's living zero," with half-
unconscious, half-unravelled sediment of bone, poison, and the
"sun that coughs and spits its lungs out," yet creates the artifice of a
new soil sensible to the miracle of genesis but also, within
untamable cosmos, to 'age-old dreads' (in the Jamaican Rastafarian
sense).

The growth of Caribbean literature is undoubtedly a
phenomenon existing against a background of a philistine middle-
class establishment. Philistinism is a much more complex state of
mind than one first thinks and possesses unique elements in the
Caribbean. It is also the natural *persona* humanity wears in a
dangerous world, it is a way of playing safe, it is a way of taking no
risks. Philistinism appears in unlikely guises, in sophisticated lies,
sophisticated laughter and debunkings of mental image or
creativity. The denial of profound exile, the refusal to perceive its
own dismembered psychical world, is basic to Caribbean
philistinism. It has led to a body of education which describes,
feasts upon, rather than participates in, the activity of knowledge.
Knowledge is imported technology (rather than 'experimental' art
or science). Indeed the term 'experimental' is used by Philistine
establishment not to imply the necessities of concentration upon
asymmetric reality but to endorse suspicions of the creative
imagination.

There are, needless to say, difficulties in assessing properly what
is meant by 'experiment' (a term B. S. Johnson tended, quite rightly

perhaps, to discourage because he saw how it could be used to belittle a writer's considered work) in imaginative writing. It needs to be said—though this is implicit in this study—that the experimental conception signifies, in our explorations, a profound, intuitively concentrated penetration of isolated functions that may seem efficient in their own right but are oblivious of joint catastrophe (and therefore of joint therapy) until it is too late. Tolstoy's *War and Peace*, which most educated West Indians regard as a towering European classic, is written in the form of documentary realism but it raises to our attention the notion of 'accidental design' in order to discredit Napoleon's 'planned victories'. By and large, the significance of the shadow of uncertainty this casts over Tolstoy's age tends to be overlooked, because that shadow does not affect the *shape* of Tolstoy's narrative in itself. It exists in the realm of 'idea' rather than active or intuitive ingredient in the form of narrative. Such a tone is, however, unmistakably at work in Claude Simon's *The Flanders Road*, where character emerges from the unconscious sediment of history raised by almost involuntary degrees into consciousness to bring about quite different narrative illuminations than one associates with the function of documentary realism.

Recalling Simon's work helps to make clear that our coinage of the term 'accidental design' requires us to focus on a body of writing which secretes parallels into infinity and a deeper comprehension of genesis within isolated worlds. From the standpoint of documentary realism, the rebuttal of planned design can be entertained as basically pure idea within a largely conventional and predictable narrative order—it can be used as ideological principle with which to chasten the paranoia of genius. But paradoxically within a narrative, intuitive strategy that is immersed in so-called accident, a complex vision emerges that sees through 'accident' into an asymmetric field in which universal character possesses its surprised roots.

Otherwise—and this is sadly the case in the Caribbean—the unity of the world comes to signify involuntarily a deposit with which an institution clothes itself to foster the appearances rather than the truths of order. The political consequences may be judged in the increasing violence of Caribbean factions that seek to pre-empt 'order' when elections occur.

If it is Europe-oriented 'one world', the deposit may train itself to conform to an inventory of books and paintings and inventions that advertise a particular brand of ideology which changes nothing—as if Europe herself were a fixed and regimented idea (if not a dead institution). If it is India-oriented, the deposit may train itself to conform to world-weary dignity that is resigned to disorder even as it voids investigations into the anguish of experiment. If it is Africa-oriented, the deposit may turn strident within fashionable black militancy, but is just as hollow in creative or evolutionary consequences. 'Modern African literature' is political ammunition rather than a cultural challenge in depth. African masks are little more than ideological weaponry, now that they have been endorsed as phenomena of genius in the museums of the West. They perform with photographic glosses in American and other Western magazines to declare "black is beautiful." Césaire's "Bantu ugliness" becomes an irrelevance; its bearing on the necessity to unlearn ways of seeing and to perceive that meaningful distortions influence the creation of every artifice of beauty is lost in a fashionable, however militant, political climate that extinguishes the shock of perception in favor of collective habit.

The habit in the region of assembling bodies of knowledge in coercive identity tends to make innovative scholarship of critical distinction and historic daring, such as C.L.R. James's *The Black Jacobins*[3] or Kenneth Ramchand's *Introduction to the Study of West Indian Literature*,[4] a rare occurrence: it is agreed, amongst sensitive scholars, that that habit contributes to impoverished dialogue with the past which one sees, for example, in the dismissive attitude toward pre-Columbian and Amerindian cultures.

There are collections of Amerindian artefact throughout the West Indies but, as I discovered when I was writer-in-residence at the University of the West Indies in 1970, and on a lecture tour in 1978, West Indian Arawak legacies are regarded as basically irrelevant to, or lacking in significance for, the late twentieth-century Caribbean. As a consequence one finds that even in the Guianas, where a living Amerindian presence survives in precarious numbers that include South American Arawaks, Macusis, Arekunas, Wapishanas, Warraus, amongst other ancient American peoples, the approach of imaginative literature to the past remains (with one or two notable exceptions) exercises in transcribing extant Amerindian legend first compiled, in the main, by European missionaries and travellers in the nineteenth and early twentieth centuries. Such transcriptions are dressed up in verse or in fiction, and are undoubtedly a valuable reinforcement of neglected materials, but it is rare to come upon original work based on such materials to match, for example, the validity of *Couvade*, a play by Michael Gilkes.[5]

The paradoxes of Caribbean age make for rich and complex realities, but these are in pawn to fake liberalisms and philistine establishments. There do exist the outlines of cross-cultural anthropology through North, Central and South America, as noted in previous explorations in this study of intuitive *rapport* with untamable myth in works such as Edgar Poe's *Pym*, Ralph Ellison's *Invisible Man*, and Jean Rhys's *Wide Sargasso Sea*, but such outlines need to be scanned with daring and integrity, with complex faith in imaginative truth—gifts that at best can now be but uneasily exercised in the Caribbean, until a radical change takes place in the prevailing authoritarian economic and political climate.

Derek Walcott's *Origins* is a brilliant poem which bears upon the problematic funeral and processional bodies of knowledge that inevitably conspire with philistinism in the West Indies. The long poem carries an epigraph by Césaire and begins by weaving an elaborate tapestry

> The flowering breaker detonates its surf.
> . . .
> Foetus of plankton, I remember nothing.[6]

Origins, therefore, begins with illusions to vacant memory and, in the same token, to namelessness. Those allusions imply that the human "foetus of plankton" is a thread within the loom of non-memory to secrete perhaps unconscious knowledge that runs far deeper than convention. Unconscious seed or "plankton" in the womb of space comprehends the subtlest beginnings of life and may, in certain imaginative contexts, shake the frame of dead matter that "lazy volumes" consolidate.

Such a reading of Walcott's *Origins* recalls our previous

emphasis upon unspectacular genesis or evolutionary epicentre. Such imaginative epicentre in *Origins* floats or is suspended in annals or lazy volumes that wash the shores of place and time. The poem's stress upon lazy volumes may arouse us to reflect afresh, I think, upon inertia or passivity of mind that spawns technologies and hollow epitaphs. No wonder the Arawaks, or any drowned agriculturalists of a past age, float or lie under a sentence of history that judges them unable to "grasp infinity" or to possess knowledge of metals.

This epitaph upon the Arawaks is curiously suspended in the poem's sensuous loom or tapestry as in a cloud, a half-sorrowful half-celebrative shadow of light, that bathes the entire poem and raises a veiled question mark against judgements based on conventional bias arbitrarily seeking to close gaps or vacancies of memory. The vanished West Indian Arawaks to whom *Origins* refers are as extinct today as the Caribs of Yurokon. Their South American cousins survive precariously in the Guianas, in Brazil, and in Venezuela.

Is the poem complexly involved in a subtle repudiation of arbitrary codes of knowledge that exploit gaps or vacancies of memory?

Is the poem immersed in unravellings of lazy volumes and biased epitaphs?

The subtle intensity of such unravellings comes to a curious head amidst tapestries of ancient Egypt, Africa and ancient Greece when foetus of ocean is misted over by the features of epic seafarer. That mist hangs between what is partially visible and what is in eclipse. Thus a mist-featured Caribbean Odysseus floats in Penelope's loom.[7] Each thread is subject to varieties of implicit re-dress that subsist on fractions rather than integers of destiny. Odysseus's potential homecoming is a marriage of past and present, a celebration of imperfect origins. Penelope's loom reflects upon half-epic, half-vacant, cradle as much as upon epic marriage bed. Each static epitaph or rumour of doomed hero or lost husband becomes *inversely prophetic*. Inverse factor or rumour implies a higher, eclipsed value. Absence implies the stored joys of reunion. Inverse epitaph implies a compensating, raised sarcophagus above a line of fate that divides numeral from numeral. It is as if a secretion of unconscious knowledge lies at the heart of problematic origins to bring to fruition what has been banished or eclipsed in death as in life.

Within twelve years of the publication of *Origins*, the scenario had radically changed into an Arawak homecoming and tribute of fame. By then Fred Olsen's *On the Trail of the Arawaks* had appeared.[8] Archeologists will decide, in the long run, on Olsen's discoveries in the West Indian island of Antigua and the emphasis he places on the puzzling question of the origins of the Arawaks, their probable links with pre-Columbian Ecuador and Peru. New questions may well be raised about the validity of this new picture, but the implications it illumines are searching enough to uncover a new dimension in Arawak achievement. Highly aesthetic pottery constitutes a parallel with some of the most well-known cultures of pre-Columbian America.

The notion of potential twentieth-century epic is an elusive yet vital strand that we have pursued in 'the womb of space'. It would be wrong to attempt a final summary within the ongoing and changing illuminations that we ravel and unravel here, but on occasion we may remind ourselves of the varying stresses of perception in half-blind, half-deaf aspects of particular works that are conscripted by collective 'imperatives', or by siren fascinations, until they are subtly re-dressed within the cross-cultural web, subtly enriched within and against other apparently alien imaginations which gain also in themselves and in their works by re-visionary interpretations that they too undergo in cross-cultural context. Indeed, each work complexly and peculiarly revises another and is inwardly revised in turn in profound context.

All this constitutes a capacity for *coniunctio* and potential for true marriage between cultures.

We have sought to pursue such capacity at a time when literature is still constrained by regional and other conventional but suffocating categories. Before proceeding to implications in the work of other poets from the Caribbean and elsewhere, I would like to make this another occasion in which to seek re-visionary counsel on cross-cultural loom in respect of the core of artifice that has cast its inner shadow upon the problematic museums and lazy volumes in the Caribbean psyche.

Walcott's funeral-origins march with Césaire's zero re-dress. Staggered associations drawn from "blind memory" in the long poem *Origins*[9] may be re-visioned against Césaire's inner "sun" and the Yeatsian "dying animal" re-dressed into "hammered gold."

Césaire dreams of Africa in returning to his native land, Columbus dreams of India in sighting unseeingly ancient (or was it a ghost of polarised modern) America. The Arawaks he misconceived have vanished. How much, yet how little, has changed in blind ghettos of poverty and wealth! To sail to Byzantium is to confront, in figures of gold or wood or stone or clay, one's blind, deaf hopes and dreams of immortality or paradise: a blindness and deafness that others also need to confront and to perceive, to unravel—even as they themselves in unravelling the past are unravelled by the past in the present and the future—and thus all achievement, however outstanding, is strangely painted or sculpted upon the very edge of non-sensibility (non-sensible gold, non-sensible wood or tree, non-sensible clay or stone).

Should non-sensible money or institution triumph absolutely, then the epic variables would apparently be aborted by hard-hearted artifice or greed or lust. On the other hand, we have seen that the mystery of alchemy and grace remains the unfathomable catalyst of the depths in the heights available to the human imagination in every circumstance.

African Pantheon

The authoritarian hand that fell upon Nigeria in the wake of her Civil War was lifted in the 1970s; a new era began to dawn even as other terrifying events unfolded. The butcher Amin fell but atrocities committed in his regime left grave scars upon the body-politic of Uganda. Zimbabwe-Rhodesia gained independence under black majority vote. The Republic of South Africa under white minority rule continued to exercise its repressive laws and obdurate functions and to highlight itself as the 'white tribe of Africa' amongst 'black tribes' that were less equipped with military hardware.

This is but a partially sketched scenario to emphasise implicitly the phenomenon of modern African literature. Its apparent fragility enhances essential, individual humanity imperilled by a framework of tribal legacies and exploitative technologies. Much stress has been laid on the collective genius or collective function of African poetry by eminent writers, such as the late Janheinz Jahn, but I tend to agree with Gerald Moore that "this does not seem especially true, except to the extent that it is true of all good poetry—do not all poets speak for mankind?"[10] And furthermore, in an age when mankind, alas, trades upon aggression in its collective entertainments and regimented body, it would seem necessary, to say the least, for intuitive genius to witness to currencies of mind and originality that are vulnerable, yet beyond material price in human order.

My question is, with respect to the Caribbean: how does the essential and numinous frailty of African poetry bear upon black West Indian writers of the last decade or two? I restrict my inquiry to the Barbadian-born poet Edward Kamau Brathwaite, but hope that the intuitive substance of what we encounter will possess echoes for readers in other, unspoken, Caribbean materials. I have chosen Brathwaite partly because of the nature of his work and the *rapport* he has sought with Africa where he lived and taught, I believe, for several years before returning to the West Indies. First I would like to look at an example of 'fragility' or numinous frailty in the work of Christopher Okigbo, one of the most gifted Nigerian poets, killed in the Civil War. Some of his poems in *Heavensgate* appear, with hindsight, almost prophetic. There is a cluster of motifs around loss of flesh, descent into the stream of being, streamsong's "blinded heron" or drowned "moonman." The poet dwells upon a singer who goes "under the shade."[11]

These poems bring home, I think, Okigbo's acute sensibility and absorption of European and African elements. The fertile spirit of poems is African—streamsong turns into shade—even as we hear Eliot's voice with its speculation on submerged houses in parallel with implicit lament of the hills

The dancers are all gone under the hill.[12]

The echoes that Okigbo cultivates with effect have the force to imbue drowned moonman with spectral houses and architectures, with shades of song that outline every vanished dancer. African pantheon subsists, therefore, on transitional chords as old as the elements into which ancient civilisations, ancient Greece, ancient

Rome, ancient Africa, tend to vanish, yet are never entirely lost within the mediating shadow and mystery of art.

Shadow or shade is alive with voices so real, yet strangely beyond material hearing, that they are peculiarly *visualised* or 'seen' in the intricate passages of a poem. *Visualised presence* acquires therefore both a *shadow and a voice* that belongs to the mind's ear and eye. The singer under the sea is lit by the moonman. Perhaps they are one and the same, moonman and singer, falling or flying in the ocean-sky of a "blinded heron."

It is in this context that I wish to approach Edward Brathwaite's poem *Jah*, the first remarkable poem in his long epic entitled *Islands*, part of an impressive trilogy *The Arrivants*.

> the ship sails, slips on banana
> peel water, eating the dark men.[13]

Brathwaite's 'music' and 'dance of death' is an original variation upon Okigbo's and Eliot's 'dancer/moonman/singer that goes under the shade'.

The poem protests the fate of eaten men and strings its protest into another shadow or "frigged-up soul." Brathwaite's fine reading performances of his poems bring home the 'jazz' variables he cultivates. Less conscious, perhaps, is he of the numinous dialectic that subsists upon visualisations of ascent and descent. *Islands* confesses to its "stopped bridge," reminiscent of Okigbo's "blinded heron." The bridge stops in the air not only of New York but of *Jah* (Jamaican Rastafarian Jehovah). The air darkens into a 'blue note' or 'cracked note' in which a borderline appears between 'jazz' and Okigban 'shade under the sea'.[14]

Brathwaite's intention to make his poems immediately available to an audience when he gives his readings can, I find, exact a penalty when the social message becomes so banal it deprives the poem of numinous shadow. The god Legba, for instance, in the poem *Legba*, is equated with a series of folk-deprivations and illnesses: pot-bellied children intermingled with maimed creatures and with black and brown people who are enslaved by banks, books and insurance businesses.[15]

Legba becomes indistinguishable from ruling deprivations. Perhaps this is legitimate as social realism, but one needs to confess that a force for radical innovation departs with such shadowless structure. The protest imagery tends to eclipse the phenomenon of formidable interior essence. Legba forfeits his complex reality when he ceases to be a daemon of inner re-dress, when his investiture and the mask he wears becomes so literal that it cannot move a people into complex authority and originality by which to fissure block institutions and create necessary economies and architectures within the soil of an endangered, polarised, yet interdependent world.

Something of numinous shadow returns to the poem when it stresses wilderness equation of the god with the plight of his people. In that context of 'wilderness-artifice' the poem achieves subtle, luminous distributions of illusion and anguish in the fall of a plantation age draping its blanket of drought upon an unfree people.[16]

We speculated earlier upon metaphoric imagery that intricately conveys music as the shadow of vanished but visualised presences. The musical associations seem therefore part and parcel of a body that echoes at such depth that it deepens our perceptions of losses and gains. Jean-Joseph Rabéarivelo of Madagascar, one of the most gifted and remarkable African poets whose tragic death by suicide occurred in 1937, creates an intuitive drum of light-in-darkness. The *sound* or *fathomless* shadow of the drum is sevenfold, the drum is fashioned from the stretched hide of a slain creature whose beat, beating hide, beating drum, turns into glittering incantation, glittering shadow of the sun's "river of light." First comes the authenticity of "hide" of the flayed creature who secretes light with its last breath in the silent lament of the drum; the secretion of light is the silent incantation, the silent question of shadowed womb of space—"But who has killed the black cow?" Then comes the arousal of "the sounding box of the wind/that is sculptured by the spirits of sleep" to dream of fathomless place, fathomless river, in cosmic drum.[17] Rabéarivelo's paradoxical 'hide of animal' recalls both *Nightwood's* 'river of sorrows' and *Gormenghast's* Flay.

In sharpest concert and paradox, Wole Soyinka's poem *Death in the Dawn* raises the deceptions a Narcissus of the folk may play on himself in slaughter that mimics sacrifice, journeys that confine him within a "futile rite."[18] The quenchings of light by light may prove to be no endorsement of clarity. The way back or the way forward exists but is dangerous for the suicidal ego. The distance to be covered "waits famished." How many eaten souls lie between death in the dawn and the original substance or goal of complex beauty the traveller seeks by which he is confused to barter all that he holds dear and "to wake the silent markets?" The hunger of time, the greed of time, he carries in himself may reflect/project him into the jaws of a mirror that becomes "the famished road." *Death in the Dawn* is a cryptic poem reminiscent of Cyclopean nightmare except that the cave of birth has become the "famished road" presided over by the mother of life and death who prays for the one who is embarking but may find himself locked in a "closed contortion."[19]

Fossil and Psyche

It is legitimate to conceive of nature poetry as seeking to realise a verbal snapshot of unchanging tree or mental stamp of flower or beast, unchanging in that the poem is convinced it sees nature as it truly is; it has caught perhaps an exact moment in seasonal manifestation, a high-point in the cycle to which tree or beast or flower returns timelessly year after year in the manuscript of place. Such exactitude becomes a design to outlast the seasons and to confirm the rhythm of passing time, yet changeless pattern. This is a beguiling conception, profoundly moving and worthwhile. But such exactitude is a fossil apparition. The fire of autumn that inscribes itself into a dead leaf to look brilliant and alive is a foretaste of winter, and forecasts the caged, if not dead, sun.

Where then does the true origin of perceived nature lie—does it lie in fossil high-point, or does it lie in masked seed and untamable fire? Does winter burn with the sun to reflect the masked fertility or seed of spring? Or does the seed obversely or reversely, in opposition to fire, mimic mausolea of ancient ice ages? Do obverse and reverse faces and nameless currencies inscribed upon seed as upon fire, upon ice, as upon every element, disclose an epicentre as unfathomable as it is unspectacular, through which the climates of the globe have erupted and changed into deserts where forests once stood, into gardens or rainforests or orchids where the sea once stood, into dry land where lakes once pillowed the sky?

In these questions glimmers the theatre of million-year-old psyche of the human animal, a glimmer of the dress and re-dress that mutated beast, mutated angel, wears. That dress tends to fossilise into a naturalistic code that pre-empts, through unconscious ironies of pigmented death or glaze of brilliant colour, obverse or reverse currencies of fertility. Such a code is eternally seductive, it compels because it successfully exploits regimes of self-pity and addiction to ornament and epitaph. Bias becomes bliss within the seduction of fossils that harden into, rather than cultivate the re-dress of, coffined cradle or timeless artefact. In that cradle humanity dissects the mummies of desert peoples or river folk, wooden peasants or iron dukes, ancient curses of Pharaoh or modern cults of Lenin. These glosses upon conscripted personality woven from histories and poetries of fossil high-point so clothe our minds that it may come as a shock to discover in them the formidable regime of the stereotype that rules civilisations.

Even in an age as rich and diverse as ours, in which masses of tourists stream from country to country, continent to continent, the changing scenery that unfolds tends to bore as it possesses the eye like cinematic decor. The mind is already constrained by what it wants to see, the hollow glamour of rich worlds or the endemic poverty of starving peoples. Nothing easily changes. Theatre is achieved around which the emotions freeze into the stalemate of the sun that encloses itself in summer beachwear or 'artifice' *that the stereotyped creature does not perceive as such*: there lies the joke, the assumption that artificial human exhibition or abandon is genuine freedom.

The balance in so-called nature between 'nature' as frozen, however hidden imperative, and 'nature' as true, elemental thaw, is not a seasonal 'given' in the human animal, attuned unconsciously to ingrained stereotype (whatever its artificial emancipation), but much more—if it is realised at all—a state of subtle, creative disruption of apparently everlasting inner codes. We spoke earlier of the blood of artifice within the body-epic, body of gold in Byzantium, a body that stands on the borderline between sensibility and non-sensibility. Is *Sailing to Byzantium* a revolutionary nature poem in its perception of artifice, its self-critical anguish and acceptance of borderlines? Is it here perhaps—in league with poets like Césaire—that the significance of a new nature poetry begins to emerge?

I would suggest that that significance resides in conditions of exile that subtly disrupt fossil ego or eternal stalemate, fashion-plate (if not stalemate) sun. The golden butterfly becomes as partial as the hackneyed sail that is apparently motionless upon a marble ocean. The balanced artifice of nature—stalemate sun, sail as pinned butterfly, butterfly as photogenic mask upon flesh-and-blood—may suddenly unfreeze into miraculous beauty within contrasting stillnesses that unsettle each other.

That unsettlement is rooted in paradox and in auction block histories, it is rooted in centuries of the conquest of species in nature, it is rooted in the conversion of conquistadorial biases into the humour of finity and infinity. Schoolchildren in the West Indies used to write quite naturally and innocently, it seemed, of English snow and Wordsworthian daffodils that they had never seen, rather than palm-groves or cane-fields or rainforests. The absurdity has often (and rightly so) been quoted as a caveat of blindness inculcated by colonial institutions stereotyped and bound within other cultural landscapes. What has been equally overlooked by zealous educationists is the unconscious humour of infinity that is written into the soil of history whose nature slides as much into snow as into galactic prairie and sevenfold shadow in Jean-Joseph Rabéarivelo's poem.

St.-John Perse, the Martiniquan-born poet, has written an astonishing poem called *Snows* in which "strange alliances . . . white nuptials of noctuids, white festivals of mayflies"[20] may come into attunement, on cross-cultural loom, with Rabéarivelo's 'flayed hide' flowered with stars.

The humour of snow in *rapport* with deceptive transparencies and constellations of cosmic beast is symptomatic, I think, of a new nature poetry. It would be fascinating to trace such 'nature-art' in imaginations under various stresses of exile or subtly disrupted stereotype. How profoundly has such nature poetry been a form of half-mystical, half-physical humour in refugee peoples around the globe?

Indians and Pakistanis, amongst other Asians, are rooted peoples, in cultural terms; their ancestral homelands still possess greatly unchanged, caste-oriented, institutional structures, underpinned by non-evolutionary assumptions, as we saw in our discussion of Raja Rao's *The Serpent and the Rope*. As a consequence, the acquisition of new roots is bound to sustain deceiving stases as well as contrivance, hand-in-hand, as it were, with unconscious artifice. I intend to glance at this phenomenon and its meaning for a new nature poetry in the poems of the gifted Pakistani-born writer Zulfikar Ghose. It may be possible to trace this matter in other Asian poets-in-exile, for example, in Caribbean Indian poets whose grandparents came from India, but the assumption is too tentative to press too far.

Zulfikar Ghose emigrated to England from Pakistan and India in 1952, long before the wave of emigration to Great Britain that one associates with the 1970s. In 1970 Ghose moved to the United States where he now lives. So, in effect, he has traversed an entire arc. The poem *Friends* is a good example not only of his early work in England but of the tendencies I wish to trace. A cluster of motifs presents itself in *Friends* (tips, fags, discreet behaviour, etc.) as comedy-of-manners soil of an ambiguous garden. In that garden, conversation and cash become "drink" for a thirsty being, drink or rain that edges into "songs of birds."[21]

A similar paradox appears in a poem called *An Attachment to the Sun* where, in tune with the winter ice on a window, the poet sees a flight of glow-worms "breathe" in a woman's eyes. One is reminded of St.-John Perse's "mistletoe feast" and "palm-groves under [winter icicle or] glass." The sensuous magical quality of glow-worms is faintly edged with nightmare as the poem proceeds with its Christmas celebration and turns from glow-worm eyes to the crack of walnuts to invoke lizards clicking "their tongues in her mouth."[22]

Indeed, however insistent the plea the poem makes for the laughter of love and for exact images of celebrative design, one begins to sense a hidden chasm of memory that persists in the soil of newly-wed place. Take, for instance, *The Lost Culture*, written in Ghose's English phase, in which urban, nightmare hollow deepens; the poem contemplates "empty lift-shaft[s]."[23]

That apparently climactic hollow grows out of a series of associations involved with clouds like goatskin bags, the "soot" of space, implicit rituals of ascent and descent masked by urban structures. The urban mask settles, yet lifts to flash into being "salmon," dream-fish, "quiet as blood." Here again—as with "songs of birds"—one edges into an implicit garden of nature. Nevertheless the shroud remains. It is peculiarly cast over everything that seems buried in space—"sooty space"—and the realism of the poem, its depiction of architectural or vehicular model, becomes deceptive threshold into memorials of ecstasy.

Church spires, Boeings descending, are in counterpoint to levitation rituals of the ancient East. Thus an unsettling character is implicitly cultivated within every contrived, apparently real model of place. The 'invisible grave' at the heart of Ghose's poem is, I think, of significance: what the poem depicts possesses another reality that needs to be seen differently, and the humour of finity and infinity runs half-despairing, half-hoping, to create new roots, new soil, out of *convertible* hollows, convertible chasms, of memory. Man-hole, lift-shaft, plane-treed avenue, all are masks for 'nature imageries' that secrete a plea for the spring of confused, darkened hope in a world that tends to wither within and without the exiled self.

Such half-stifled 'nature' masked by technology is alien to conventional expectations and the poet himself needs to wrestle with a borderline logic that may lead into a dead-end. The very precision of structure in the poems seems to belie the shroud of the past that drapes them and drapes their innermost hollow. Furthermore, that precision is beguiling for it possesses the seductive pull of stasis within Eastern pictorial legacies.

Take an ancient Chinese print; its definition deceives and may even be exploited to give an exotic flavour to twentieth-century magazine and pictorial advertisement, which is raised thereby to aerial fossil certitude. Convert this predilection into a tension between 'fossil high-point masked by technology' *and* 'invisible shroud', and it gives us some indication, I believe, of the underlying, subconscious or unconscious stresses in Ghose's poems that give them their sharpest mood and pathos imbued with brilliance and edged with sculpted or hidden eyes.

In *The Lost Culture* we draw close to those hidden eyes. With dry yet bitter humour we are led into London's Tate Gallery to ponder a shallow and profound counterpoint in squiggles upon a painter's canvas. Van Gogh's crows were also squiggles over graven, dazzling cornfields, and the poem recalls the blind pupil or "gouge[d]" eye of a child in Bombay, India.[24]

Before he leaves England for America, the poet's ambivalent affair with spirit of memory and place embroiders a meditation on 'vision' to revive the uncertain prospect of 'garden of nature', live, fossil, sensuous roots, secret rendezvous for lovers, a pond in whose stillness "my eyes are stars." A curious ghostly balance now appears between 'gouged eye' and "air's mouth" to give anatomy of space to a moment of reflection.[25]

In Zulfikar Ghose's first American poems, *The Violent West*, anatomy of space seems both to harden and atrophy in an arid garden.[26] And it is by degrees, in later work, that arid time changes and dazzled eye deepens. *A Memory of Asia* secretes a new and profound current that has its roots in "water's edge" as in "moon[s] torn from the Pacific" to fertilise "opaque transparencies."[27]

The capacity to convert, rather than succumb to, deprivations is one of the strands that we have pursued in 'the womb of space'. The shock of the cross-cultural web is the humour of finity and infinity. Yeats's Byzantium is present in Pablo Neruda's *Macchu Picchu* in the line, "famine, coral of mankind."[28] How close is Neruda's "coral of mankind" to "whales grazing sargasso" in the fine poem by Trinidadian poet Wayne Brown?

> The mountain squats suddenly at your ear, so close.[29]

We have sought to raise many questions in this exploration. The dangers that encompass humanity are undeniable but within them the echo of transformative capacity lives to deepen our responses to inner and outer hazards, inner endangered space, outer endangered space. To convert rooted deprivations into complex parables of freedom and truth is a formidable but not hopeless task. The basis of our inquiry lies in the conception that one may address oneself to diverse fictions and poetries as if they are the art of a universal genius hidden everywhere in dual rather than monolithic presence, in the mystery of innovative imagination that transforms concepts of mutuality and unity, and which needs to appear in ceaseless dialogue between cultures if it is to turn away from a world habituated to the pre-emptive strike of conquistadorial ego.

The voice of authentic self is complex muse of otherness:

> O you singer solitary, singing by yourself, projecting me,
> O solitary me listening, never more shall I cease perpetuating you.[30]

Notes

Introduction

1. Alfred Métraux, *Voodoo in Haiti* (London: Andre Deutsch, 1972).
2. Alastair Hannay, *Mental Images* (London: George Allen & Unwin, 1971).

Chapter One

1. Edmond L. Volpe, *William Faulkner* (London: Thames & Hudson, 1964).
2. William Faulkner, *Intruder in the Dust* (London: Penguin in association with Chatto & Windus, 1960), p. 208.
3. Ibid., p. 7.
4. Ibid., p. 8.
5. Ibid., p. 10.
6. Ibid., pp. 15;16.
7. Ibid., pp. 85-86.
8. Ibid., pp. 148-150.

Chapter Two

1. Edgar Allan Poe, *Arthur Gordon Pym of Nantucket* (New York: Hill and Wang, 1960).

2. Ibid., p. xxv.
3. Ibid., pp. 10; 16; 18; 42.
4. Ibid., p. 16.
5. Ibid., p.8.
6. Ibid., pp. 18; 42.
7. Ibid., pp. 42-43.
8. Ibid., pp. 70-74; 88-90.
9. Ibid., p. 169.
10. Walter Roth, *Animism and Folklore in the Guiana Indians* (Washington, D.C.: Bureau of Ethnology, 1909).
11. Ibid.
12. Richard Schomburgk, *Travels in British Guiana* (London, n.p., 1848).
13. Michael Swan, *The Marches of El Dorado* (London: Jonathan Cape, 1958), pp. 284, 285.

Chapter Three

1. Ralph Ellison, *Invisible Man* (New York: Vintage Books, 1972), p. 3.
2. Ibid., p. 3.
3. Ibid., p. 12.
4. Ibid., pp. 27; 25.
5. Ibid., pp. 226; 463.
6. Ibid., p. 11.
7. Ibid., pp. 126-131.
8. Ibid., pp. 62-63.
9. Ibid., p. 242.
10. Ibid., pp. 57-58.
11. Jean Toomer, *Cane* (New York: Harper & Row, 1969).
12. Ibid., p. 108.
13. Ibid., p. 116.
14. Ibid., pp. 126-127.
15. Ibid., p. 128.
16. Ibid., p. 129.

Chapter Four

1. Robert B. Stepto, *From Behind the Veil* (Champaign: University of Illinois Press, 1979).
2. Ibid., pp. 172-173.
3. Juan Rulfo, *Pedro Páramo* (New York: Grove Press, 1959); Selden Rodman's review appeared in the *N. Y. Times Book Review*, June 7, 1959, p. 5.

4. Ibid., pp. 5-6.

5. Ibid., p. 113.

6. Ibid., p. 5.

7. Ibid., pp. 9-10.

8. Ibid., p. 117.

9. Michel Foucault, *Les mots et les choses* (Paris: Gallimard, 1966).

10. Jay Wright, *The Double Invention of Komo* (Austin: University of Texas Press, 1980).

11. Ibid., p. 3.

12. Ibid., p. 4.

13. Ibid., p. 23.

14. Ibid., pp. 13; 15-16.

15. Ibid., pp. 64-65.

16. Ibid., p. 45.

17. Jean Rhys, *Wide Sargasso Sea* (New York: Popular Library, 1966).

18. Ibid., p. 189.

19. Ibid., pp. 113-114.

20. Ibid., pp. 86; 189.

21. Ibid., pp. 54; 60-61.

22. Ibid., p. 61.

Chapter Five

1. Paule Marshall, *The Chosen Place, the Timeless People* (London: Longman, 1970), p. 6.

2. Ibid., p. 3.

3. Ibid., p. 11.

4. Ibid., p. 11.

5. Ibid., p. 17.

6. Ibid., p. 12.

7. Ibid., pp. 274-275.

8. Ibid., p. 366.

9. Ibid., pp. 367; 472.

10. Patrick White, *Voss* (London: Penguin Books, 1960), p. 89.

11. Ibid., p. 90.

12. Ibid., pp. 445;444.

13. Ibid., p. 144.

14. Ibid., p. 148.

15. Ibid., p. 149.

16. Ibid., pp. 243; 244.

17. Ibid., p. 379.

18. Ibid., pp. 377-378.

19. Ibid., p. 379.

20. Raja Rao, *The Serpent and the Rope* (London: John Murray, 1960).

21. Ibid., p. 7.

22. Ibid., p. 7.

23. Ibid., p. 8.

24. Ibid., p. 9.

25. Ibid., pp. 384-385.

Chapter Six

1. T. S. Eliot, *Selected Prose* (London: Penguin Books in association with Faber and Faber, 1953), p. 154.

2. Mervyn Peake, *Gormenghast* (New York: Ballantine Books, 1968).

3. Ibid., pp. 2; 1.

4. Ibid., pp. 1-2.

5. Ibid., p. 3.

6. Ibid., pp. 94-95.

7. Ibid., p. 95.

8. Ibid., p. 3.

9. Ibid., pp. 94; 1.

10. Ibid., pp. 94; 6 and 166; 4.

11. Ibid., pp. 6; 7.

12. Théophile Gautier, *Portraits et souvenirs littéraires* (Paris: Charpentier, 1881, translation by G. L. Van Roosbroeck in *The Legend of the Decadents*, Columbia University, 1927).

13. Charles Baudelaire, *Oeuvres completes* (Paris: Pleiade, n.d.).

14. Jean Toomer, *Cane* (New York: Harper & Row, 1969), p. 32.

15. Ibid., p. 33.

16. Mervyn Peake, *Gormenghast* (New York: Ballantine Books, 1968), pp. 6; 4.

17. Ibid., p. 30.

18. Ibid., p. 167.

19. Ibid., p. 168.

20. Ibid., pp. 166; 11.

21. Ibid., p. 168.

22. Ibid., pp. 11; 22.

23. Ibid., p. 14.

24. Ibid., pp. 168; 161.

25. Ibid., p. 170.

26. Ibid., p. 22.

27. Ibid., pp. 19-20.

28. Emma Tennant, *The Last of the Country House Murders* (London: Jonathan Cape, 1974).

29. Ibid., pp. 77-78.

30. Ibid., p. 79.

31. Ibid., p. 75.

32. Ibid., p. 79 and p. 95.

33. Ibid., pp. 96-97.

34. Ibid., p. 122.

35. Claude Simon, *The Flanders Road* (London: Jonathan Cape, translated by Richard Howard, 1962).

36. Ibid., p. 27.

37. Ibid., p. 26.

38. Ibid., p. 27.

39. Ibid., p. 13.

40. Ibid., pp. 44-46.

41. Ibid., p. 53.

42. Ibid., p. 42.

43. Ibid., p. 14.

44. Ibid., p. 43.

45. Ibid., p. 14.

46. Djuna Barnes, *Nightwood* (London: Faber and Faber, 1937).

47. Ibid., p. 210.

48. Ibid., p. 182.

48. Ibid., p. 182.

49. Ibid., pp. 231; 227.

50. Ibid., pp. 154; 162-163; 191.

51. Ibid., p. 192.

Chapter Seven

1. Aimé Césaire, *Return to My Native Land* (London: Penguin, translated by John Berger and Anna Bostock, 1969), pp. 56-58.

2. W. B. Yeats, *Selected Poetry* (London: Macmillan, edited by A. Norman Jeffares, 1962), p. 104.

3. C.L.R. James, *The Black Jacobins* (London: Allison & Busby, 1980).

4. Kenneth Ramchand, *Introduction to the Study of West Indian Literature* (London: Nelson, 1976).

5. Michael Gilkes, *Couvade* (London: Longman, 1974.).

6. Derek Walcott, *Selected Poems* (New York: Farrar, Straus, & Co., 1962), p. 51.

7. Ibid., p. 54.

8. Fred Olsen, *On the Trail of the Arawaks* (Norman: University of Oklahoma Press, 1974).

9. Derek Walcott, *Selected Poems* (New York: Farrar, Straus, & Co., 1962), pp. 52-54.

10. Gerald Moore, ed., *Modern African Poetry* (London: Penguin Library, 1963), p. 21.

11. Ibid., p. 105.

12. T. S. Eliot, *Four Quartets* (London: Faber and Faber, 1959), p. 27.

13. Edward Kamau Brathwaite, *Islands* (London: Oxford University Press, 1969), p. 3.

14. Ibid., p. 3.

15. Ibid., pp. 15-16.

16. Ibid., pp. 16-17.

17. Gerald Moore, ed., *Modern African Poetry* (London: Penguin Library, 1963), pp. 33-34.

18. Ibid., p. 112.

19. Ibid., pp. 112-113.

20. St.-John Perse, *Exile* (New York: Pantheon Books, translated by Denis Devlin, 1949), p. 83.

21. Zulfikar Ghose, *Penguin Modern Poets 25* (London: Penguin, 1975), p. 79.

22. Ibid., p. 81.

23. Ibid., p. 85.

24. Ibid., pp. 85-86.

25. Ibid., p. 75.

26. Zulfikar Ghose, *The Violent West* (London: Macmillan, 1972).

27. Zulfikar Ghose, "A Memory of Asia" *Sun*, vol. 4, no. 3 (Winter 1979-80), p. 81.

28. Pablo Neruda, *The Heights of Macchu Picchu* (London: Jonathan Cape, translated by Nathaniel Tarn, 1966), p. 41.

29. Wayne Brown, *On the Coast* (London: Andre Deutsch, 1972), p. 7.

30. Charles T. Davis and Gary Wilson Allen, eds., *Walt Whitman's Poems* (New York: New York University Press, 1955).

Bibliography

Barnes, Djuna, *Nightwood*. London, Faber and Faber, 1937.

Baudelaire, Charles. *Oeuvres complètes*. Paris: Pleiade.

Benston, Kimberly, W. *Baraka*. New Haven and London: Yale University Press, 1976.

Brathwaite, Edward Kamau. *Islands*. London: Oxford University Press, 1969.

Brown, Wayne. *On the Coast*. London: Andre Deutsch, 1972.

Césaire, Aimé. *Return to My Native Land*. Translated by John Berger and Anna Bostock. London: Penguin, 1969.

Cooke, Michael G. *Acts of Inclusion*. New Haven and London: Yale University Press, 1979.

Davis, Charles T., and Gay Wilson Allen, eds. *Walt Whitman's Poems*. New York: New York University Press, 1955.

Ehrenzweig, Anton. *The Hidden Order of Art*. Berkeley: University of California Press, 1967.

Eliot, T. S. *Four Quartets*. London: Faber and Faber, 1959.

Ellison, Ralph. *Invisible Man*. New York: Vintage Books, 1972.

Faulkner, William. *Intruder in the Dust*. London: Penguin in association with Chatto & Windus, 1960.

Foucault, Michel. *Les mots et les choses*. Paris: Gallimard, 1966.

Gautier, Théophile. *Portraits et souvenirs littéraires*. Paris: Charpentier, 1881. Translated by G. L. Van Roosbroeck. In *The Legend of the Decadents*, Columbia University, 1927.

Ghose, Zulfikar. *Penguin Modern Poets 25*. London: Penguin, 1975.

_____. *The Violent West*. London: Macmillan, 1972.

Gilkes, Michael. *Couvade*. London: Longman, 1974.

_____. *West Indian Fiction*. Boston: G. K. Hall, 1981.

Hannay, Alastair. *Mental Images*. London: George Allen & Unwin, 1971.

Harris, Wilson. *Tradition, the Writer and Society*. London: New Beacon Books, 1967.

_____. *Explorations*. Aarhus, Denmark: Dangaroo Press, 1981.

James, C.L.R. *The Black Jacobins*. London: Allison & Busby, 1980.

James, Louis. *The Islands in Between*. London: Oxford University Press, 1968.

Jung, C. G. *Psychology and Alchemy*. Princeton, N. J.: Princeton University Press, 1968.

King, Bruce. *The New English Literatures*. London: Macmillan, 1980.

Maes-Jelinek, Hena. *The Naked Design*. Aarhus, Denmark: Dangaroo Press, 1976.

_____. *York Notes, Heart of Darkness*. London: Longman, 1982.

_____. *Wilson Harris*. Boston: G. K. Hall, 1982.

Marshall, Paule, *The Chosen Place, the Timeless People*. London: Longman, 1970.

Métraux, Alfred. *Voodoo in Haiti*. London: Andre Deutsch, 1972.

Moore, Gerald, and Ulli Beier, eds. *Modern Poetry from Africa*. London: Penguin Library, 1963.

Moore, Gerald. *The Chosen Tongue*. London: Longman, 1969.

Neruda, Pablo. *The Heights of Macchu Picchu*. Translated by Nathaniel Tarn. London: Jonathon Cape, 1966.

Olsen, Fred. *On the Trail of the Arawaks*. Norman: University of Oklahoma Press, 1974.

Peake, Mervyn. *Gormenghast*. New York: Ballantine Books, 1968.

Perse, St.-John. *Exile*. Translated by Denis Devlin. New York: Pantheon Books, 1949.

Poe, Edgar Allan. *Arthur Gordon Pym of Nantucket*. New York: Hill and Wang, 1960.

Ramchand, Kenneth. *Introduction to the Study of West Indian Literature*. London: Nelson, 1976.

Rao, Raja. *The Serpent and the Rope*. London: John Murray, 1960.

Rhys, Jean. *Wide Sargasso Sea*. New York: Popular Library, 1966.

Roth, Walter. *Animism and Folklore in the Guiana Indians*. Washington, D.C.: Bureau of Ethnology, 1909.

Rulfo, Juan. *Pedro Páramo*. New York: Grove Press, 1959.

Rutherford, Anna, and Kirsten Holst Petersen. *The Enigma of Values*. Aarhus, Denmark: Dangaroo Press, 1975.

Schomburgk, Richard. *Travels in British Guiana*. London: n.p., 1848.

Simon, Claude. *The Flanders Road*. Translated by Richard Howard. London: Jonathan Cape, 1962.

Stepto, Robert B. *From Behind the Veil.* Champaign: University of
    Illinois Press, 1979.
Swan, Michael. *The Marches of El Dorado.* London: Jonathan Cape, 1958.
Tennant, Emma. *The Last of the Country House Murders.* London:
    Jonathan Cape, 1974.
Toomer, Jean. *Cane.* New York: Harper & Row, 1969.
Volpe, Edmond L. *William Faulkner.* London: Thames & Hudson, 1964.
Walcott, Derek. *Selected Poems.* New York: Farrar, Straus, & Co., 1962.
White, Patrick. *Voss.* London: Penguin Books, 1960.
Wright, Jay. *The Double Invention of Komo.* Austin: University of
    Texas Press, 1980.
Yeats, W. B. *Selected Poetry.* Edited by A. Norman Jeffares. London:
    Macmillan, 1962.

Index

Ramchand, Kenneth, 124, 146
Rhys, Jean, xv, xvi, 76, 125, 141,
    146; *Wide Sargasso Sea*, 49-54,
    56, 58, 59, 61, 66, 71
Roth, Walter, 24, 51, 140, 146
Rulfo, Juan, xv, 103, 140-141,
    146; *Pedro Páramo*, 40-46,
    68, 69

Schomburgk, Richard, 24, 140,
    146
Simon, Claude, xv, 143, 146;
    The Flanders Road, 107-113,
    123
Soyinka, Wole, 119, 131-132, 146
Swan, Michael, 24, 140, 146

Tennant, Emma, xv, 120, 142-
    143, 146; *The Last of the
    Country House Murders*,
    102-106
Therapy: and cataclysm, as con-
    version of block functions, 108-
    110; and the uninhabited angel,
    117

Toomer, Jean, xv, 46, 140, 142,
    146; *Cane*, 34-38, 40, 44, 94-
    95, 109-110
Twinships: in relation to *Pym*,
    20-21; in relation to Yurokon,
    25

Voodoo: within *expédition* or
    l'envoi morts, xiii-xv; within
    Caribbean catholicity, 52-53;
    within mask of *hungan* in
    Gormenghast, 98-99
Volpe, Edmond L., 4, 12, 146

Walcott, Derek, xv, 143, 146;
    Origins, 125-128
Wells, H. G., xi
White, Patrick, xvi, 141, 146; *Voss*,
    66-78
Whitman, Walt, 137
Wright, Jay, xv, 40, 141, 146; *The
    Double Invention of Komo*,
    48-49, 55-56

Yeats, W. B., 119, 121-122, 128,
    137, 143, 146
Yurokon, 24

About the Author

WILSON HARRIS is Visiting Professor at the University of Texas
at Austin and Regents' Lecturer at the University of California.
He has held positions at the University of the West Indies, the
University of Toronto, Leeds University, the University of Mysore,
Yale University, and the University of Newcastle, Australia.
An internationally known novelist, he is the author of *The Angel
at the Gate*, *Palace of the Peacock*, *Explorations*, *The Tree of the
Sun*, and many other books.